The Freedom We Crave

ADDICTION: THE HUMAN CONDITION

WILLIAM LENTERS

GRAND RAPIDS, MICHIGAN
WILLIAM B. EERDMANS PUBLISHING COMPANY

Copyright ©1985 by Wm. B. Eerdmans Publishing Company
255 Jefferson S.E., Grand Rapids, Mich. 49503

Library of Congress Cataloging in Publication Data

Lenters, William, 1941-
   The freedom we crave.

   1. Compulsive behavior. 2. Substance abuse.
I. Title.
RC533.L46   1985   616.89   85-10339

ISBN 0-8028-3602-X

Contents

2-5-86 psy/drk

Preface

Here is the warning which the law requires as a companion now for each new shipment of amphetamine as it leaves the factory:

"Amphetamine has been extremely abused. Tolerance, extreme psychological dependence, and severe social disability have occurred. There are reports of patients who have increased dosages to many times that recommended. Abrupt cessation following prolonged high dosage results in extreme fatigue and mental depression; changes are also noted in the sleep and EEG. Manifestations of chronic intoxication with amphetamine include severe dermatoses, marked insomnia, irritability, hyperactivity, and personality changes. The most severe manifestation of chronic intoxication is psychosis, often indistinguishable from schizophrenia."

Want some?

The late 20th century will go down in history, I'm sure as an era of pharmaceutical buffoonery.[1]

The problem of addiction in our culture is not a drug or alcohol problem, but a people problem. That, stated briefly, is the thread that runs through this book, both in our description of the causes and characteristics of addiction and in our suggestions for starting on the road to recovery. The chilling warning Kurt Vonnegut quotes above may scare a few people away from amphetamines, but addiction kits are everywhere.

Our purpose is not to add another self-help book to the already crowded racks, coining catchy and absurd slogans like "Drugs do not kill people, people do." Nor will we join our voice to the chorus of those who lambast the beverage alcohol industry and wallop the pharmaceutical companies with easy moralisms about the evils of demon rum and tranquilizers. Although the whole story of the risk factors in alcohol consumption or the prescribed use of other mind-altering drugs remains to be told, we are not going to try to finish it here.

No, the often completely untold story of addiction is really the drama of the human spirit responding to the stress of life. This is our focus. Our concern is with people, with how they develop addictive patterns of living to cope with existence, and with freedom from addiction. Our hope is that through these pages addicted persons and those seeking to help them can find some pointers to "Recovery Road" and freedom from the prison guaranteed them by their "habit." Perhaps the freedom we crave can become the freedom we celebrate.

The
Freedom
We
Crave

CHAPTER I

Addiction and the Human Condition

Jerry is the sixth son of immigrant parents. As he was growing up, his father's strict, churchgoing Calvinism set the tone for family life. Jerry learned his catechism lessons, joined the church, attended worship services every Sunday (usually twice) and midweek meetings in between.

The family was strict, but they were not teetotalers. Table wine was common at their meals, and as Jerry grew older he enjoyed an occasional beer with his friends.

Following high school, Jerry went off to college, eventually becoming an engineer after graduation. He married, fathered a child, bought and furnished a modest but comfortable home in the suburbs. He owns a home computer and a video-recorder for his television set.

In short, an apparently straightforward and ordinary life: no skeletons hidden away in the closet of his past, no hidden secrets, no signs of trouble on the horizon.

But Jerry develops a drinking problem. Eventually his heavy drinking breaks up his marriage, alienates him from his family and from the church and community in which he grew up. Once too often he shows up late for work with liquor on his breath, and he loses his job. More and more he has started to contemplate suicide as the only way out.

Jerry could not drink without becoming intoxicated. Eventually he could not *not* drink; that is, he lost his power to choose. Every occasion turned into an occasion for a drink. In the eyes of many people, he has become a victim (or a perpetrator) of a disease called *alcoholism,* a disease covered by Blue Cross and Blue Shield.

Ostracized by family and friends, terminated by his employer, divorced by his wife, Jerry has come to be one of a breed apart, pigeonholed by those acquainted with him as just another of thirteen million or so alcoholics in the United States. Jerry is an addict.

Alcoholics and other drug addicts are people whose psychosocial and metabolic reactions to a mind-altering drug are different from those of the great majority of the drinking and using population. Jerry and people like him cause fatal traffic accidents, reduce productivity in industry by millions of dollars each year, contribute to the erosion of family structures, send insurance rates skyrocketing.

When we see Jerry or someone like him, our immediate reaction may be to think "Thank God I'm not like one of *them.*"

That—to state it baldly—is rubbish. We *are* like one of them. The Jerrys of this world became everybody else's scapegoat, but they mirror the image of all of us. The trail of tragedy that persons addicted to alcohol or other drugs leave behind may tempt us to project the problem of addiction exclusively on them. But that tactic—whether it makes us feel self-righteous or merely fortunate—simply will not work.

A major contention of this book is that addiction describes something that happens to everyone at the deepest level. None of us is exempt. All have fallen short of the freedom we crave. Our symptoms may be more repressed or subdued than Jerry's; the path of unhappiness we tread more subtle. No one need notice. But the addiction experience is the human experience, not the monopoly of a boisterous or boozy 10 percent of the drinking population. We all weave our own behavior patterns and habitually repeat that which provides and secures relief and escape. We may all spell "relief" in our own way, but we all spell it some way. The human project includes passing through the crucible of addiction. Because everyone seeks safety, salvation, purpose, and meaning, we are all vulnerable to the addictive process.

Some people, like Jerry, are addicted to behavior patterns which have a serious adverse effect on the lives of several other people. Helping such persons would be a much simpler matter if addiction were a simple matter. As our attempt to set out an adequate theory of addiction will demonstrate, it is not.

The questions are many and puzzling. Addiction *to what?* Is addiction a disease? Is it a sin? Is it a psychological abnormality? Does it point to a personality disorder? A moral weakness? A physiological anomaly? A genetic mix-up? Are addicts morally responsible for their frequent foul-ups? Is addiction a case of obsessive-compulsive behavior? Or is it just an excuse for anti-social behavior? What causes one person to become addicted to beverage alcohol while his biological brother does not? Is every addiction harmful? What about the so-called positive addictions?

But the primary goal of this book is not to answer such questions with yet another theory of addiction. Its goal is to provide a strategy for recovery from addiction, a way out of the addictive trap, a resolution, or perhaps a process toward freedom from addiction.

Sound strategy, however, requires good theory. Recovering alcoholics who sponsor newcomers to the program of Alcoholics Anonymous repeat the refrain, "Action is the magic word. You need to walk the talk." True. Good words by themselves do not result in recovery. Nevertheless, the program of Alcoholics Anonymous is itself based on sound theory and presuppositions, elaborated in the first five chapters of the *Big Book of Alcoholics Anonymous.*[1]

Along the way, readers may find themselves reevaluating if not abandoning some of their stereotypical images of the addicted person. No one's story is "typical"—not Jerry's, not yours, not mine. Each of us is unique. Our stories have similarities, but they also disclose what is special and singularly "I" and "mine."

We will elaborate on our contention that everyone is vulnerable to the addictive process by considering what it means to be human. We shall be paying particular attention to a dimension of human nature that theologians identify as "sin" and psychologists refer to as personality or character disorder. A central question is this: "How do we cope with existence? How do we live and not simply survive? How do we deal with the sense of being finite and with the limits of our existence?" One answer: We cope inadequately, sinfully, neurotically. We develop almost ritualistic behavior patterns. Our personalities take shape around the habits we thoughtlessly cultivate.

Addiction, however, penetrates further than behavior patterns. Who we are at the deepest level of our beings discloses an addictive personality structure. The stuff of our existence is shot through with the makings of harmfully repetitive and habitual patterns.

Human beings tend to be predictable, not fickle. That is why psychology can claim to be a science of understanding human behavior and the human spirit rather than merely the art of knowing people. What explains this phenomenon of changelessness in human existence?

People do not change at the deepest level of their being without an outside intervention. A recent book by B. Zilbergeld develops this point.[2] People do not change their ways or improve their neurological lot via the costly route of psychotherapy. For the most part, says Zilbergeld, we hang on to our hang-ups. The gimmicks and games, the heroic efforts of willpower, the magic of religious ritual or the suddenness of radical and momentary conversion: does any of them offer a consistent promise of authentic recovery that will alter our inner self and consequently our outward action? Can we reshuffle our emotional deck of cards and successfully come up with a new deal?

Emotional sleight of hand and relational bluff may lure one into believing that personality changes can happen that easily. But although freedom from addiction is possible, the freed person is never free at the deepest level. He or she can never return to the object of obsession because it has never been left entirely behind. As is said at Alcoholics Anonymous meetings, "Once you've been pickled, you can never go back to becoming a cucumber."

Recently I visited a congregation I had served ten years earlier, on the occasion of its twenty-fifth anniversary. It had been my first pastoral charge. I loved those people—and I still do. During long conversations with old friends it became apparent that problems then were problems now. Old Jack never had learned to deal healthfully with his chronic back pain. Poor Jim was as cynical as ever, turning thumbs down on any suggestion of trusting other members of the body of believers. Jane was still neurotically affected, fearful of being misunderstood and unloved. Franky's double-barreled righteous indignation was still aimed at the morally unhinged and the theological illiterates who rummaged about in what he calls pious trivia. And Karen was as depressed as she had been a decade ago.

Yet my ministry there made a difference! I was reminded of a story Billy Graham had told a group of us would-be preachers during a seminary conference: "I was confronted by a drunk in an aisle on a crowded airplane. There was no avoiding him. He stopped me to tell me how grateful he was for my ministry and how my preaching had changed his life. And then he turned away and bobbed and weaved his way back to his seat." Similarly, these people from my first congregation thanked me profusely for the work God had done in them through me. Why wasn't the grace of power to heal the hurts more apparent? Where was the grace of forgiveness to absolve the guilty tears once and for all? Where was the grace of promise to sweeten sour spirits?

This book is not meant to be negative nattering against the hope of recovery. But in the effort to speak with some realism about the prospects for recovery, we shall have to expose the fantasy in the quick but temporary "fixes" that line the self-help shelves at your local bookstore.

A further clarification: this book does not try to unravel the mystery of what psychologists call obsessive-compulsive personality disorders. Obsessive-compulsive behavior is only a corner of the issue. The study of it is a study of personality *disorder;* our concern with addiction as the human experience makes this book—in part at least—a study of *personality.* Alcohol addiction, for instance, can be studied from the perspective of obsessive-compulsive disorders, but we will be considering it as just one case of human addiction. Not all human beings are addicted to beverage alcohol, but all human beings are compulsively attached to one or more particular forms of a patterned existence.

We shall focus our discussion on three of these behavior patterns which often lead to a full-blown addictive process: romantic love relationships, beverage alcohol consumption, and religious practice. In addition, we will take a brief look at three others: fitness, food, and work.

Sex, the use of ethanol, and religion do not always set up addictive patterns in people. They are not, therefore, always harmful or dangerous or immoral. But because addictive life-styles are often reflected in these areas of human existence, lovers, drinkers, and strong believers may be putting themselves at risk.

Some addictive practices are obviously more debilitating and destructive than others. But all addiction is to some extent harmful. To make that claim contradicts a prevalent spirit in contemporary American culture, sometimes described by the term *positive addiction*.[3] That is an appealing idea only if one disregards the possibility that someone who is "high on the positive" may be under the spell or control of a resource outside himself or herself. I would contend that external objects of obsession are harmful in themselves because they rob us of that essential freedom which is ours as human beings.

If, for example, my love for the game of racquetball becomes obsessive, it becomes harmful, even if it is having notably positive effects on my physical and mental condition. The crimp in the family budget, missed appointments, schedule reshuffling, late arrival at the family dinner table—all are annoying and sometimes painful consequences I must face squarely and honestly. But the heart of the matter is the loss of choice I experience. This approaches what is truly harmful about all addictive behavior. To paraphrase the first answer of the Heidelberg Catechism, I am no longer my own, but belong—body and soul—to my favorite obsession. The core issue in my addiction to racquetball is that the game has in effect rendered me powerless to choose to play or not to play. I must play—or suffer withdrawal symptoms.

This may seem like a fairly insignificant example, but every addiction is characterized by such an experience of powerlessness. In this book we will be discussing the dynamics of powerlessness and the paradox of responsibility in the face of powerlessness and loss of choice. We will face the paradox of human freedom and the ambiguities of the human condition.

Is there hope for the human condition? Can a person overcome addiction? If not, my task in this book would be a fruitless one. But there is hope. I have witnessed, known, and worked with scores of people who were once "hopelessly" addicted and are now enjoying the taste of new wine, celebrating recovery and newly found freedom. They are in process of realizing that hope is also a here-and-now reality, not just a heavenly reward somewhere off in the future.

Too often religious responses seem to treat hope as something ethereal, eternal, surreal, or simply fantastic. If that were all there is to it, in Ogden Nash's phrase, "Hope would be dope." Hope in God is not hope that is dope. But hope in God must be translated into the realities of the here and now, in terms that bring a tangible peace to lives boxed in by patterns, routines, and habits. Hope that is entirely futuristic is not hope but illusionary fluff.

Hope for the addict means freedom from addiction *today*. Only a life with authentic options freely chosen is authentic life. But freedom from a compulsive behavior and freedom to choose between alternatives must not lead in turn to an addiction to those alternatives—as sometimes happens with people who become therapy addicts, or "A.A. junkies," or religious fanatics. Nor is this freedom without paradox, for no freedom is total or absolute.

Readers will thus find no panacea in these pages. There are no cure-alls, no offers of grace without responsibility, no easy "how to's," no moralisms to help you on your way. You will not discover the secret of how to be your own best friend or to pull your own strings. The freedom spoken about throughout this book is freedom grounded in the good news that God was in Christ reconciling the world to himself. It is a freedom there for the asking, a freedom we can only receive, not a freedom won or a freedom bought or a freedom earned. It is a freedom given and a freedom received.

So lay down your religious tool kits. Put away the psychobabble. Dispense with your almighty willpower. There are no steps to take *toward* freedom, though there are steps to take *in* freedom. I want to unpackage the mystery of grace while guarding that ineluctable and ineffable gift.

The availability of that gift means that an addict does not have to be forever cabined within the framework of his or her genetic hold. Addicts need not be the perpetual victims of their own personal holocaust. We don't have to be tied for all time to the monotonous rail of repetition, predictably tracking a course already set before us.

In the next chapter we will consider the human experience in terms of its vulnerability to an addictive process. Then three separate chapters will look at the dynamics of love and addiction, ethanol and addiction, religion and addiction. Following these is a brief chapter devoted to some "other" addictions—fitness, food, and work. Finally, we will outline a strategy of recovery from addiction and an experience of freedom.

CHAPTER II

Addiction: The Human Experience

C. S. Lewis's novel *Perelandra* has a vivid passage in which he describes how the main character, Ransom, wakes up to the intoxicating sights and smells of the imaginary world from which the book takes its name:

> Looking at a fine cluster of the bubbles which hung above his head he thought how easy it would be to get up and plunge oneself through the whole lot of them and to feel, all at once, that magical refreshment multiplied tenfold. But he was restrained. . . . He had always disliked the people who encored a favourite air in the opera—"That just spoils it" had been his comment. But this now appeared to him as a principle of far wider application and deeper moment. This itch to have things over again, as if life were a film that could be unrolled twice or even made to work backwards . . . was it possibly the root of all evil? No: of course the love of money was called that. But money itself—perhaps one valued it chiefly as a defence against chance, a security for being able to have things over again, a means of arresting the unrolling of the film.[1]

That vignette by Lewis touches a reality that is at the core of human experience. Like Ransom, everyone craves both the security of repetition and the euphoria of intense refreshment. But not everyone succeeds in confronting this twin passion.

This itch to "do it" and "do it again" comes from deep within the spirit. Whatever the "it" may be, one hungers for the rush of intense feeling, the flush of pleasure. It may come from a piece of forbidden fruit, or the first sexual drum roll in the hay of adolescence, or the first chemical high from alcohol or "speed" or marijuana. It may even happen on an evening at Comiskey Park in response to Billy Graham's passionate invitation to come to the Savior.

What is this itch to feel so *damned* good? What is it that pushes us beyond the melancholy routine of duty? St. Paul's description in Romans 7 of that tortured soul on the horns of a dilemma between feeling good and doing good is an analysis of Everyman's itch in theological terms.[2] The "right stuff" is all there: we want to do what is good; we want to fulfil our calling. At the very same time, we want to satisfy our longing for the euphoria of an altered ego state, an intense sensation of pleasure, an orgasmic peak that rises to the occasion.

The picture in Romans 7 is of a person caught moving in a southerly direction on a northbound street, simultaneously feeling the push to get out of the way before being plowed under by oncoming traffic and the daring rush of excitement to beat the odds and bull his way through. What is that dominant force that keeps us kicking against the standards of conventionality? To call it the weakness of the flesh or casually to flip out the "sinful nature" coinage fails to do justice to what is in fact powerlessness to resist the urge to fly free of restraint.

Let us see how the phenomenon of addiction can be described in terms of yielding to an itch for euphoria, an itch over against which we are virtually powerless.

Dominant among the complex factors that make up this itch is *powerlessness*. Writing to the Galatians, Paul speaks of a man *caught up* in a trespass (6:1). The picture of powerlessness that comes to mind is one of a fly entangled in a spider web—a buzz of frantic spinning and turning going nowhere. Freedom's paradise is lost. What is it about a person that causes him or her to give up personal freedom, the power to choose between alternatives, and offer himself or herself up to an obsession? What are these controlling and devouring "gods of the belly" (Philippians 3:10)?

A walk on the wild side has an attractively alluring aura. St. Augustine recognized that, looking back on his youthful shoplifting extravaganzas as motivated by sheer joy at the theft itself:

Theft is punished by the law, O Lord, and the law is written in the hearts of men, which iniquity itself effaces not. For what thief will abide a thief? Not even a rich thief, one stealing through want. Yet I lusted to thieve, and did it compelled by no hunger nor poverty but through a pamperedness of iniquity. For I stole that of which I had enough and much better. Nor cared I to enjoy what I stole, but joyed in the theft and the sin itself. A pear tree there was near our vineyard, laden with fruit tempting neither for color nor taste. . . . And this, but to do what we liked *only because it was misliked.*[3]

Augustine experienced a pulsating high when he stole pears. Except for the declining number of young people growing up in rural areas, that might be difficult to understand. But we understand only too well that what turned him on was not the fruit ("tempting neither for color nor taste") but the act of doing that which was judged to be a moral wrong ("only because it was misliked"). Sinning—not just *sin*—is fun. It is grand sport to "raise hell."

The high of adolescent experience need not be a chemical one. Often it is simply the thrill of the chase, the excitement of going out of bounds. It may be stealing a kiss, polishing off a six-pack with the boys in the graveyard, or pumping B-B pellets at Old Man Lazzarro's window pane. No mind-altering drugs need be ingested, although there is a hormonal high the youthful offender gets simply from doing what is "misliked." The adrenaline is pumped. The adventure lies in barely getting away without being found out. The high is *almost* getting caught with your hand in the proverbial cookie jar. The young adventurer beats the gods at their own game. The misdeed itself is only incidental to the feeling that it generates.

The adolescent experience of Augustine is similar to everyone's adolescent storm and stress. We have all kicked with healthy exuberance at the parental goads and codes that stood in the way of our rambunctious self-becoming-self. It is somehow part of the youthful task of self-definition and separation from the parental cast. The rub comes in the form of a new dependency—the idolization of the adolescent experience. One might also observe that the adolescent experience of addiction is more a matter of fixation than full-blown addiction, a dependency easily and quickly remedied because of the malleability and flexibility of the young. Adolescents heal quickly.

Nevertheless, this does not minimize the seriousness of the dependency. There is what is called in psychological jargon an object-cathexis, in which a person becomes neurotically attached to someone else or to a pattern of behavior for no other reason than an emotional "fix." "It feels so damned good." Feeling good is the *summum bonum* of adolescence. Alas, far too many adults remain in adolescence.

A walk on the edge of adventure illustrates our proneness to addiction. Adventure helps to satisfy the itch; but it must be adventure that comes close to violating a moral standard which judges behavior as right or wrong, good or bad. Augustine flogs himself verbally for going one step beyond that which is simply human. Confessing his desire to love and be loved in return, he chides himself for the way this reflected his sinful human nature. Listen to him practically talk himself out of God's gift.

> What was it that I delighted in, but to love and be loved? But I kept not the measure of love of mind to mind, friendship's bright boundary: but out of the muddy concupiscence of the flesh and the bubblings of youth, mists fumed up which beclouded and overcast my heart, that I could not discern the clear brightness of love from the fog of lustfulness.[4]

Augustine is not complaining about sexual awareness but about his fixation on his sexuality and what his sexuality produced within the network of his felt emotional needs. His obsession with his sexuality was lustful concupiscence.

For centuries human beings failed to distinguish between awareness of their sexuality and obsession with it. Some would have, if possible, exorcised all sexual feeling. They confused natural sexual desire with lust, thus branding sexuality as unholy and wholly unnatural when in fact, because we are embodied selves, it is wholly human and natural. What is unholy and wholly unnatural is our fixation on and then our addiction to our sexuality.

Our generation, enlightened as it is about the "joy of sex," is mesmerized and obsessed by sexual expression as a "fix." As a result, ours is a generation that has deprived itself of much that is thoroughly enjoyable about sexuality. What comes naturally and freely we distort with undue emphasis on the mechanics, techniques, and gymnastics we suppose will enhance it. Here lies the paradox: we are drawn to expressing ourselves sexually. We pursue that passion hotly. But then that to which we are naturally drawn becomes that on which we are hooked. Addiction.

Although sexually enlightened and confident that we express our sexuality with more gusto and brilliance than earlier generations, we have not really extricated ourselves from Augustine's problems. We still experience guilt for our sexuality. Preoccupation with sexuality seems to be closely related to guilt about it. The one feeds the other: that for which I feel guilty is the very thing to which I am drawn. We will discuss addictive sexuality in more detail in the next chapter. Here our focus is this process of becoming fixated on an object of fascination, fun, and feeling (in this instance, our sexuality) *because we perceive it as morally reprehensible.* The simple fascination of pursuing a perceived moral wrong becomes intensified, obsessive, even pathological. We become addicted to that which makes us feel guilty. The high is generated in the experience of doing that for which I will be judged guilty and might accordingly be punished. The extreme case of such addiction is the criminally insane psychopathic person.

As a moth is attracted to the "bug" light, the addict is drawn to that which he or she perceives as morally wrong. There is a fascination with guilt that produces a sense of euphoria. This is sick. This is addiction. It is also very human.

To understand the obstacles and resistance human beings set up to the grace of recovery, restoration, and rebirth, we must push beneath the surface of such traditional theological terms as the "reprobate heart," and try to unpack some of the dynamics of our restless, wandering selves, our urge for feeling guilty. Feeling guilty is feeling high. A poignant example is the alcoholic on Skid Row, for whom guilt is the sustaining protein of life. The binges, one after another, powerfully reinforce a self-image of worthlessness and rottenness. The down-and-out alcoholic is hooked to feeling guilty, unhooked from the feeling of responsibility. The addiction to alcohol facilitates the more profound fascination of freedom from accountability. The helpless captive of his or her loss of accountability, such a person experiences guilt but is powerless to do anything about it.

This description of the Skid Row alcoholic's dilemma is not intended to ignore or deny the other dimensions of addiction to beverage alcohol, but to suggest that a significant factor in the dynamics of addiction is the way in which guilt feelings are used as neurotic tools to perpetuate an irresponsible life-style. Guilt feelings paralyze rather than set free. They tend to lock in behavior patterns. The dog returns to his vomit. Why? He simply does.

Guilt feelings enhance the obsession with the behavior patterns that induce the guilt. We capitulate to the enemy in our drive to overcome the enemy by way of the feeling of guilt. It all begins in apparently harmless fashion: a little "relief" drinking followed by a slight, dimly felt sense of guilt ("I let myself down"). This feeling of guilt is assuaged by more "relief" drinking. That is the insanity of alcoholism—the paradigm of addiction. The one feeds the other.

There is within us a natural temptation to suppose that feeling guilty will somehow enable us to overcome our guilty behavior and thereby, with one swoop, wash away all our guilty stains. In fact, it intensifies the attraction to the repetitive behavior and the accompanying feeling of guilt.

Nowhere do the Scriptures command us to *feel* guilty. They only declare that we *are* guilty. This declaration that we have fallen short of God's expectations is a legal description of our relationship with God. A right relationship with God is not restored through a feeling of guilt; nor is habitual behavior overcome through a heroic and independent effort of sheer willpower. Restoration with God comes through the grace of God. The legwork on our part is to say "yes" to the divine "yes."

Paul Tournier makes a helpful distinction between true guilt and false guilt.[5] True guilt reflects a violation of moral law. Awareness of true guilt is the mark of a healthy spirit yearning to be free from the bondage of disobedience. It is guilt grounded in grace. False guilt is entangled in the web of the fantasy that restoration with God is the product of a do-it-yourself moral facelift. It is the fine paid for deserting yesterday's sacred cow.

All of this points to a critically important and universally human dynamic of addictions: the paradox of freedom. To understand compulsive addictive behavior we must take account of personal human freedom, a master key that unlocks the mystery of being human. Let me begin by setting forth my presupposition that human beings are created in the image of God. Because we bear the divine image, we have the privilege and the responsibility of freedom.

Freedom has an inalienable negative aspect: freedom *from*.[6] This is the freedom of independence, of not-being-dependent. The freedom of independence allows me to walk on the wild side, to let the restless wind that is in me blow. I am free to sow my oats, to risk, to scratch where I itch, to be guilty, to sin. I am free to feel the ecstasy of experience, to stand as it were outside of my own limitations and look down on what I have created with my experience. Like God I am free to bless my work and say, "Behold, it is very good!" I am free from the divine "ought" laid on me by my Creator.

But I am free only to a point. I am not absolutely free. Absolute freedom would mean immunity or exemption from every bondage, restraint, restriction, or consequence. Only God has this kind of complete freedom from everything external to himself. He is in bondage to no one and to no thing.

Human beings, created in the divine image, have creaturely freedom, which is contingent on the creative grace of the Creator. It is limited by the restraints of time, space, natural and moral law.

The tragedy of the human story is that man does not surrender to the reality of contingent freedom but rebels against the limitations that come with it. Finding contingent freedom quite intolerable, man opts for the dangerous—and ultimately impossible—task of unseating God from the throne in the name of personal freedom. That failed and failing attempt to usurp the throne creates a new trap for human freedom: obsession to escape one's bondage to moral and natural law.

Trying to overthrow God in the name of absolute freedom is not a one-shot *coup d'état:* it is usually a lengthy process. Nor does the price to be paid for it immediately fall due. There may be many moments of giddy euphoria gleaned from the illusion of sitting in the captain's chair. But during the course of insistence on absolute freedom from all restraint, one is eventually and inevitably burned by the restraints of a patterned existence and a compulsive life-style. "Absolute" freedom becomes a burden and finally a burnt-out case of futility. A tragicomic example is the "macho" egotist eager to enhance his reputation as a sexual athlete. The drive to demonstrate this prowess to as many women as possible will often lead to a humiliating and sustained bout of impotence.[7]

A more familiar example is the patterned mural of adolescent rebellion against authority and bondage to peer pressure in the name of absolute personal freedom. Obsessed with the goal of freedom, adolescents become entrapped by the very pursuit of it.

Consider this adolescent pursuit of freedom more closely. In the process of development from childhood to adolescence, there is an awareness of what Fromm calls a *growing aloneness.*[8] The child emerges alone from the dark age of pubescence, separate from others, into a world that is powerful and intimidating. There is a faintly dawning awareness that parents will not always be around to come to the rescue. This is a phenomenal childhood task.[9] But boys and girls do emerge from the cocoon. And they emerge free and spontaneous, like beautiful butterflies.

Alas, that freedom and spontaneity are short-lived. The fear of being alone and the growing sense of aloneness catapult the newly free adolescent into the hastily structured womb of the "buddy." Peer pressure is conceived; eventually conformity is born. Patterns and repetitive behavior multiply. *Everyone* is wearing designer jeans and sweaters with alligators on them.

Intoxicated by this new freedom, the adolescent may begin to feel fear and isolation when sobering up. The response is to take another swig of freedom, to force oneself into peer relationships, mindlessly following the herd into the hold of unfreedom. And thus, by conformity to the pressure of the group, born out of the anxiety of aloneness, another child is born, another son or daughter is given over to the loss of personal freedom and the human penchant for addictive behavior—all in the name of absolute freedom!

There is a kind of security in being unfree. Erich Fromm makes the political application of this psychological insight in his book *Escape From Freedom,* suggesting that by our failure to live with freedom we will probably submit to the rule of totalitarianism. But the same point can be illustrated at the personal level of the human soul tortured by bondage to a patterned existence.

Human freedom has a dialectical character. On the one hand, it is a process of growing from strength to strength, a mastery of nature, a growing power of reason, a stepping out in faith, a development of basic trust in other human beings, an increasing conviction that there are authentic choices to be made. John Steinbeck's discussion of *the choice* Adam and Eve were required to make in the garden is a marvelous account of the critical issue confronting the human being "coming of age." He had to choose. And in choosing he became free.[10] Fromm maintains that the choice Adam and Eve made together signaled the beginning of human freedom.[11] But it was negative freedom. They freed themselves from coercion. They experienced the intoxication of being *free from*.

On the other side of the dialectical dilemma, human freedom comes to expression in fear, in a growing sense of isolation, insecurity, shame, in loss of meaning and purpose in life. Stepping out alone is perceived as an attempt to unseat the Creator of the universe. The shock of this perception is enough to scare one into a flight from freedom. Unable to handle the thought of freedom, one willingly submits to another, lesser authority.

The paradox of freedom is critical to our understanding of human addiction. Addiction can be seen as a search for freedom turned in on itself. Disillusioned with the contingent freedom given at creation, we opt for absolute freedom. Unhitching the lifeline that tethers us to the mother ship, we willfully step out into the empty space created by the fantasy of absolute freedom. It's a stunning view, but there is no breathing room. In a panic to survive our failed mission, we grab on to anything that promises us breath, even if for only a few moments. Like an alcoholic in his darkened room, we reach for yet another bottle of cheap wine to numb the creeping sensation that this is the end of the line for our futile flight to freedom's paradise.

Alan Watts says that as "belief in the eternal within becomes impossible, men seek their ultimate happiness in the joys of time."[12] When a person comes to realize that absolute freedom is an illusion and the vagaries of unfreedom offer no solution, he may be attracted to God in the same way as the proverbial atheist in a foxhole. Perhaps the "God-fix" can do a sort of ambulance run for a person stuck on the treadmill of anxiety, but it will not get one to the hospital. Frustrated by the failure of the "God-fix" to provide authentic freedom, he settles for the brief intermittent joys of time. After all, as the beer advertisement reminds us, we only go around once in life, so we have to grab for all the gusto we can. The mind flits nervously from one pleasure to another without finding rest and satisfaction. There is no slaking the thirst for freedom.

Consequently, our age is, in Alan Watts's words, "one of frustration, anxiety, agitation, and addiction to 'dope.'"[13] The "dope" to which he refers is our high standard of living, with its violent stimulation of the senses, which in turn makes them less sensitive and thus in need of more stimulation. This development of *tolerance* to stimulation happens with nonchemical highs as well as chemical experiences. (How else does one explain the behavior of a prominent orthodontist, an ex-football star, who pleads guilty to a charge of counterfeiting?) We crave distraction: lights, camera, action, thrills, chills, spills, pills—anything to perpetuate the fantasy and deny truth.

In Romans 1 and 2 St. Paul describes humanity run amok. And God lets them "go to hell in a hand basket," as it were. Three times in Romans 1 (vv. 24, 26, 28), Paul repeats the refrain: "God gave them over. . . . " Chasing after an illusory freedom results in anxious filling of vacuums. The addict is stuck on the treadmill of his pursuit, denying what he knows in his heart—that he is not free—and, in this compulsive pursuit, frittering away the contingent freedom with which we are all created.

The god of this world which we have been discussing at some length is "freedom of choice." As an expression of individual autonomy and the basis of human dignity and responsibility, it is at bottom a joyless joke and a cheerless charade. Anderson says it cannot be otherwise, because it denies dependence on Another as the source of one's personhood *and* also because it is so compulsively and earnestly sought.[14]

Desperately, often angrily, the alcoholic seeks his or her freedom; but the web of addiction becomes stickier and more possessive in direct proportion to the energy devoted to that pursuit. Sometimes this pursuit of freedom comes cloaked in the guise of "perfectionism." Perfectionistic tendencies in the alcoholic are often interpreted as a psychological defense mechanism—in other words, compensation. More than likely, however, they are symptomatic of an attempt to control and manipulate the environment. The alcoholic compulsively demands perfection of himself or herself in order to have the sense of being at the computer terminal of his or her world. At some level the alcoholic knows this. The freedom to be perfect is an awesome, even impossible, responsibility. But the fantasy of perfection, the wish for it, the obsession with it remain. The alcoholic retreats into the unfreedom of the fix and takes a "hit" from ethanol in order to escape the frustration of not being absolutely free.

Fromm helps us to penetrate more deeply into this paradox. To the extent that we experience an *intermezzo* of freedom now and then, and thus become more independent and self-reliant, we also become more isolated, alone, and afraid.[15] We run to the comfort and security of one god or another to escape the terrible burden of freedom.

One result of this flight from freedom is a domesticated perversion of historic Christianity. From the comfort of our town and country estates, we boast about "freedom of worship." But we have lost the "inner capacity to have faith in anything which is not provable by the methods of the natural science."[16] The god of the natural sciences has erased our sense of wonder and, says Robert Farrar Capon, obliterates the dream and the fantasy of faith.[17] We celebrate freedom of worship, but instead of a God who sets us free to Spirit-stimulated spontaneity we bow down to one that chains us to religious ritual.

A liberated society allows—even urges on us—the freedom to dabble in the expression of any of our sexual fantasies if the price or the charm or the charisma or the chemistry is right. At the same time, there is hell to pay in terms of sexual dysfunction and breakdowns of relationships. Just ask Anthony Thrasher and Miss Doubloon of Kalamazoo—to mention only one of many examples from contemporary literature, drama, or cinema—about that.[18]

Freedom that is only freedom *from,* with no thought of freedom *for,* freedom that is compulsively sought rather than graciously received, is no freedom at all. It is a terrible burden under which those who bear it eventually stumble into the abyss of habituation. Ask any Pharisee of Jesus' day. This freedom which is grasped for is accompanied by feelings of isolation, powerlessness, and fear. They may be alleviated temporarily by one fix or another—be it ethanol, erotica, or the ethereal—but only temporarily.

This grasped-for absolute freedom is much too frightening and straightforward an awareness. So we whistle in the dark, engage in a daily round of activities, get lost in the self-affirming and ego-gratifying hustle-bustle of existence: having fun, going places, making contacts.

Theologians call this vicious pursuit of absolute freedom "sin." It is a condition that requires more than a patching up here and there; it demands that we "lay down our arms"[19] and get ready for a whole new regime. The Psalmist knew that the heart of the matter was the fetus of the matter: we are brought into being in the framework of iniquity (Psalm 51:5). Born free? Born blemished. Sin is a word for our common denominator human disorder. It is refusal to submit to a freedom that is contingent on the "givenness" of the Giver.

Our defection results in a loss of freedom brought about by the pursuit of absolute freedom. In this sense "sin" and "neurosis" are two sides of the same coin: the complete isolation of the individual, the attempt to create one's own world from within oneself, the refusal to recognize and accept one's cosmic dependence.[20] Here is the dependent infant arching the back and twisting free from Mother's arms to escape her nurturing grasp. There is the infant crawling back to Mother's arms to escape the fear of being out on his own.

Paul Tillich discussed this paradox of freedom in terms of the freedom and destiny that coexist in "essential being," that is, in a state of innocence. This freedom and destiny live within each other, distinct but not separate from one another, in tension but not in conflict. The source of their polar unity is that both are rooted in the ground of being. In a moment of *aroused* freedom, Tillich says, a process begins in which freedom becomes arbitrariness and separates itself from the destiny to which it belongs. Willful (sinful) acts are those in which freedom moves toward separation from its destiny—what Alcoholics Anonymous calls "self-will-run-riot."[21] Tillich will not let us forget this ambiguity, this polarity of our existence. The tension that exists between freedom and determinism must simply be allowed to be there. Tragedy results from attempts to resolve the polarity of autonomy and destiny.[22] One such attempted resolution is life in the fast lane. Another is apathy and premature retirement to the home for the pathologically predestinarian. Neither will resolve anything in the long run.

Reinhold Niebuhr discussed the paradox of freedom in the light of his treatment of sin as sensuality. The sensual person leads with the body. Decisions are bodily decisions: if the body feels like it, do it. Sensuality gives free rein to such a morality of the body. "Is not sensuality," asks Niebuhr, "just another form of self-love?"[23] Or is it an expression of the self-lover's feeling of inadequacy? Mere self-worship in the name of freedom turns out to be wholly unsatisfying, so the person intensifies the worship of self in the sensual world. Sensuality is as good a reinforcement for self-worship as any: it is immediate, tactile, "into pleasure." It can soothingly set free the spirit, as anyone can attest who has experienced romantic love and the suspension of anxiety while lying in the lap of sensuality.

Freeing himself or herself from restraints, the person wallows in the luxury of the far country, tantalizing every nerve ending in his body, luxuriating in the sweet smell of sensuality. "Bucks, booze, and broads." Not everyone would be quite so candid, crude, or cynical in giving expression to their goals, but these ideals of street-wise sensualism represent an "I" that lurks within all of us at one level or another. Is this freedom? Or is it, as Niebuhr suspects, another form of escape from the self? The terrible burden of freedom is too much. The person seeks to gratify the self. Though opting for self-love, he ultimately realizes that self-love is the journey of the fool discovering his own inadequacy. Paul said, "O wretched man that I am," in Romans 7. One wonders what the Prodigal Son said when he "came to himself" (Luke 15:17).

Niebuhr, like Fromm, is suggesting that absolute freedom is too hot for us to handle, and in seeking to escape we run into that which we are fleeing: a bondage to the self's gratification of self. Drunkenness, he maintains, exhibits this ambivalent end. The intoxicated person seeks the abnormal stimulus of a drug in order to experience the sense of powerful freedom denied him in his otherwise sober existence. Instead, he finds himself hooked into a cycle of powerlessness and bondage to that which would set him free. He becomes less free, not more free. "Drunkenness is merely a vivid form of the logic of sin which every heart reveals: Anxiety tempts the self to sin; the sin increases the insecurity which it was intended to alleviate until some escape from the whole tension of life is sought."[24] Once more, the treadmill of addiction.

We become free to the extent that we own and accept that we are not free, says Anderson.[25] The realization of that acceptance is a lifetime process, as we shall discuss further in Chapter 7.

The paradox of human freedom is certainly a master key to open up an understanding of human addiction. But there is one further element to our scenario of the addiction-prone self. That element is death and how we deal with it.

We cannot get out of life alive, and *that* scares us to death. We hear a good deal these days about the "stress of life." What generates that stress is anxiety about our own death. Helmut Thielicke quotes the trenchant remark by the Roman philosopher Seneca in *De Brevitate Vitae* ("On the Brevity of Life") that "It takes all of our life to learn how to die but we busy ourselves with other things."[26]

Thielicke chides our generation for dealing with death by diversion, stupefaction, and a closing of the eyes. This closing of the eyes to death becomes a life-style.[27] The media do a good job covering the stress of life our generation experiences. What gets considerably less attention is how well we cover up what rattles our addled age, the throbbing anxiety that pulsates beneath the pavement of the fast lane. The chronic hurriedness to get somewhere, the endless refrain of "I've got people to see, places to go, and things to do," is a cover-up for *the* issue of life, which is death.

Let us not be fooled by the exotic and apparently exciting pace set by the La Jolla Beach surfers in their custom-built vans loaded with laughing bronzed bodies. (Does anyone work in California? "If Dodger Stadium is not filled to capacity it is only because they are all at the beach or the race track," Harry Caray, the Chicago Cubs announcer, once observed during a road trip to the West Coast.) Let us not be hoodwinked by the apparent freedom of hang-gliding artists floating in the sky. Let us not be duped by the studied casualness of the singles bars. Here there is free and easy sex, no strings attached; smoke a little marijuana, get a little high. There is far more of the tragicomic than the cosmic here.

These cautionary notes are not meant as envious moralistic yammerings from an aging religious conservative. They are meant to suggest that the frenetic pace of our hot-tubbing, racquetball-ing, aerobic-dancing, foot-stomping, rockin' and rollin' genera-tion may look like more fun than ever before but unfortunately tends to compress itself into a sadly contrived and addicting coverup for the anxiety of life, which is anxiety about death.

Ernest Becker has written a significant book on this subject for our time. *The Denial of Death* helpfully illuminates a signifi-cant causative factor in the development of addiction.

The dust of death settles on all of us, and we cannot escape successfully beneath the canopy of denial without at the same time imprisoning ourselves within the fortress of addiction. "The idea of death, the fear of it, haunts the human animal like nothing else; it is a mainspring of human activity—activity designed largely to avoid the fatality of death, to overcome it by denying in some way that it is the final destiny for man."[28] Friends com-ment that I must be in great physical shape after playing racquet-ball five times a week. I respond silently to myself: "Just running from the Grim Reaper."

The contemporary physical fitness craze is more than a judi-cious attempt to put some balance in an otherwise Platonic mindset in regard to the body. It heaps guilt on our weary psyches for every extra pound, for that telltale middle-age "spare tire," for indulging the forbidden pleasure of strawberry pie, for that lack of regular physical exercise. We may be temples of the Lord God; we are also doomed to return to the dust. Most of us do not like that. Addiction is a response to our profound aversion to being like the grass of the field, here today and gone tomor-row.

Our pursuit of excitement and intoxication, of experiences that are immediately gratifying, sensuously stimulating, and spiri-tually uplifting, reflects our urgency to deny the reality of the ominous shadow hovering over us. Our unconscious—and some-times even conscious—hope is that we can somehow sidestep death. No one pictures himself or herself as a corpse in a casket without flinching and devising a detailed denial mechanism to handle the anxiety, usually one that is shot through with an addictive pattern characterized by anything but a surrendered state of consciousness.

Death is something you can fight but not prevail against; something you can flee, but it will catch up with you. The literature on modern health, the jazzy exercise records and sexy workout books, the miracle drugs and the back-to-the-good-earth diets—none of them owns up to how near the end is for all of us, quite apart from the spectre of nuclear conflagration. The most inevitable fact of life is that we cannot get out of it alive.

Death is of course a subject on which philosophers, theologians, and poets have reflected much. William James has framed the truth of death's inescapability as eloquently, perhaps, as anyone has: "Let sanguine healthy mindedness do its best, with its strange powers of living in the moment and ignoring and forgetting; still the evil background is really there to be thought of, and the skull grins in at the banquet."[29]

Again: "The old man, sick with an unknown disease, may laugh and quaff his wine at first, but he knows his fate now for the doctors have revealed it; and the knowledge knocks the satisfaction out of all these functions. They are partners in death and the worm is their brother, and they turn to mere flatness."[30]

And finally: "Riches take wings; fame is a breath; love is a cheat, youth and health and pleasure vanish. Can things whose end is always dust and disappointment be the real goods which our souls require? Back of everything is the great spectre of universal death, the all-encompassing blackness. The breath of the sepulchre survives it."[31]

Grim talk. But true. We handle this reality in any number of ways. We discover and invent religion with life after life or philosophize about the immortality of the soul. *Denial.* We concede that we "go around only once" so we strain for all we can get. *More denial.* We develop what Sander Ferenczi has called "secret psychoses," which show up behind the tight-lipped masks, the smiling masks, the earnest masks, the satisfied masks, that people use to bluff the world and themselves.[32] *Still more denial.*

The addicted self is responding to the shock of finitude that begins to dawn on us already in childhood. The childhood nightmare is a continuance of the struggle to survive the unknown, a struggle that first appears in the anxious panic an infant feels on being separated from the mother's breast.

Humanity must live with the existential paradox of being free yet bound, being out of nature but hopelessly tied to it. Space-craft circle the planet and touch down on the moon, but the crew members inside them are, underneath their ingeniously protective space suits, housed in heart-pumping, breath-grasping bodies whose destiny is to decay six feet below the surface of the earth. The splendid majesty of human sovereignty over all the rest of creation as a thinking, feeling, creative, relational, historical being cannot undo the reality that the human person is a worm and food for worms.

To avoid the sounds of death rumbling overhead, we retreat to a patterned existence, an addictive life-style, because in the routine of repetition there is that strange security about which C. S. Lewis writes in the passage quoted at the head of this chapter. Sameness is faithful, true, ready to provide an insulating fix that quickly and quietly mutes our painful awareness that life is terminal.

So there is more to the alcoholic's story than his or her exceptionally low pain threshold. It is more a matter of an acute awareness, even on a subconscious level, that there is a chamber of horrors at life's terminal point. The facile assumption is often that the alcoholic can't stand the heat in life's kitchen, can't face the music. Perhaps. But the alcoholic is more tuned in than most of us to the last chord. The oft-repeated near misses with the final crunch open him or her to the raw truth. "The irony of our condition is that the deepest need is to be free from the anxiety of death and annihilation; but it is life itself which awakens it, and so we must not shrink from it to be fully alive."[33] Of course we do shrink—and for many people the shrinking takes the form of drinking. But the compulsive behaviors by which we try to keep our life alive, manageable, and familiar only serve to remind us of the old folk wisdom that "the hurrieder I go, the behinder I get."

The two paradoxes of freedom and of the ultimate fragility of our fragile human condition explain at the deepest level our addiction-proneness. Resolution of our soul-sickness is possible only through the profound process of surrender and acceptance.

We will discuss this process of surrender at greater length in Chapter 7. For now it is enough to say that authentic freedom is a gift to the surrendered heart; and victory over the fatal defect is a given, the experience of which is realized in the dual acceptance of death and resurrection.

Like rocks in Hoosier farmland, the addictive life-styles that emerge and disrupt our culture keep showing up in different sizes and shapes. Three of the most familiar are romantic love, alcohol, and religion. To these we now turn.

CHAPTER III

Romance, Love, and Addiction

"Bernard Ketchum told us about one of Plato's dialogues in which the old man is asked how it felt not to be excited about sex anymore. The old man replied that it was like being allowed to dismount from a wild horse."[1]

Somewhere, at this moment, someone is painfully identifying with that sentiment. It may be a woman whose husband has just shocked her by asking for a divorce, or a young man who had discovered that the young woman with whom he was living has simply moved out, or a couple who have slid into a decision to stop seeing each other, or a newly bereaved widow or widower. Any of these people may be suffering the effects of withdrawal from an addictive relationship. The problem about which half the people in therapy complain is the difficulties experienced with a lover or a spouse or loneliness experienced because there is no lover to love.

Do not get me wrong. I am all for love. In no way am I ready to get off that "wild horse" of Plato's. On the contrary. It is my conviction that learning how to love, being competent to love, being available for love is probably the most important process that will ever engage us. Learning to love and be loved is the key which unlocks our potential to do what we ought to be doing in the world on behalf of those who suffer the trauma of hunger and fear and deprivation.

I once counseled another minister and his wife. He was an angry preacher whose sermons were long and dry and hostile.

His breath was bad, his temper volatile, his demeanor slovenly. Self-righteous and rigid, he was one of those tragic figures who know neither how to love nor how to receive love. His wife was cold, turned into herself, scarcely conscious any more that she was a person with a body. She was long past frustration over her inability to reach her husband. Yet in her quiet despair, she was bonded, even addicted to her husband. And he was to her. My experience in counseling this couple had, I am certain, a greater impact on me than it did on them. They were two people who believed in love, who had at one time in their relationship interacted romantically. Yet, here they were, cold, dead, stuck to each other, the tragic victims of a burned-out addictive relationship.

What that experience impressed on me is that all of us need to learn how to love again. We need to be available for love both in giving and receiving. What does that mean? What does it imply for us as sexual selves: how do we love appropriately with our bodies? How can I give myself in a relationship and still maintain my integrity and my freedom as a person? How can I give myself away, lose myself in love to another without losing my identity, my 'I'? How can I learn to love without addiction?

Problems arise in relationships when love is confused with addiction. What is often romantically described as "being in love" could better be called being addicted to the beloved.

If romantic love is a myth, it is not because romance is mythological. Most people fall madly in love at one time or another, whether with a real person or an idealized somebody out there. No, the mythical element is the burden that we expect romantic love to carry, the expectations we put on romance or the idealized image of it. Why were *Love Story* and its clones so successful on the paperback racks and at the box office? Because of the undying belief in the god or goddess of romance and what it is supposed to do.

The illusory expectations we have of romantic love are familiar:

● *I will be a completed person if I am in love.* After all, didn't God say that it wasn't good for a man or woman to be alone? And it is true that we are in a certain mysterious way made for the other. But to say that we are incomplete without a partner is to turn this truth on its head. At this point in a love relationship the tension between freedom and unfreedom and the terrible burden of freedom is exposed. Union with another is great, but it does not complete me to be united with another person. Union in marriage or union in romantic love is no guarantor of completeness.

• *I can address my deep sense of solitude only in a romantic liaison with another human being.* This, too, is at best a half-truth. The other half is that everyone must paddle his or her own canoe. All of us are basically alone. We live out our lives in solitaire, though not in solitary fashion. Marriage, a romantic affair, the swinging singles scene, the gay bars, the adulterous liaisons—none of these can mask the reality that I am alone and I die alone. Ernest Becker returns again and again in *The Denial of Death* to the point that the problem of life is our avoidance of the truth that we die alone. Relationships are a common unconscious form of avoiding that truth. Hence the pathos and pain at every deathbed or funeral where the partners cling desparately to each other for fear that when one dies, the other dies too.

The awareness of this solitude is also experienced painfully after a moment of sexual intimacy. So unbelievably close, and yet so far! In fact, the pain of romantic love is the pain of loneliness, because there is always the ebb and flow of coming together for a while only to be separate again. There is no final resolution; only the ebb and flow. To address the loneliness and the despair of death exclusively through a romantic liaison is to court disaster. It is much better to address my self first, to learn to live alone, to learn to live into the reality that I do live alone even as I die alone. To do so will make my relationships healthier and more open-ended. There is a parallel here between relationships and religion, as we shall see in more detail in Chapter 5. Religion becomes sick for the believer who clings to crosses and relics, rituals and formulas, because these foster dependency. Religion stays healthy when believers discover freedom, purpose, and meaning in their relationship with God.

• *Connection with another human being will resolve my anxieties, my neuroses, my traumas.* If only I had someone to share my life with, we believe, the pain would go away. The fact is, however, that entering a relationship out of a need to resolve conflicts will only intensify and compound the existing problems. The classic illustration of the pitfalls here is the woman or man who rushes into marriage to escape an unhappy parental home—only to create a new, even unhappier home.

• *Love can make me happy.* What this simple romantic cliché ignores is that *no* other person will make me happy. My happiness is a by-product of my doing some things right in my life, or living in accordance with my values, or accomplishing some task that requires of me a giving expression of my true and total self. The accent here is on *give.* To enter a relationship with someone else out of a need for happiness is in some sense to violate that other person, to take pieces from him or her in order to fill in one's own gaps.

When you take before you give, or when you give in order to get, or when you demand a response to your giving, all sense of spontaneity on the part of the beloved is snuffed out. He or she can no longer woo you but can only react to your demand for love. The magic of relationships—and much of the happiness they can bring—is because they happen as they happen.

None of this blowing the whistle on the myths of romantic love will come as a surprise to most people. Yet in spite of the contradictions, the disillusionments, the disappointments, even the despair, we go on falling in love. Romance is here to stay. And as long as it's here to stay, and as long as it's the closest approximation we have in the flesh to a quenching of that thirst, a quieting of that restlessness we feel for God, let us look more closely at some of the dynamics of romantic love, seeking some clues to how it can degenerate into something addicting and debilitating.

One of history's greatest poets, best known for his *Divine Comedy,* Dante is also remembered for his celebrated love for Beatrice. He tells us that he first fell in love with her at the age of nine. By the time he was eighteen he was deeply in love with her. But they were never engaged. There was never any sexual intimacy between them. They both married other persons. But Dante reports that he was shocked by his feelings. He describes them as a sort of stupor. The feeling of falling in love is essentially a moment of violent change, after which nothing will ever be the same again. No two people are ever the same to each other after they have been lovers.

The relationship of Dante and Beatrice highlights two out-standing features of romantic love. The first is a sense of *given-ness*. That explains the appropriateness of the expression "falling in love." Romantic feeling is a given. There is no controlling the falling or not falling; no decision to be made. It just happens. Dante could no more generate his love for Beatrice than he could generate a bolt of lightning. Once a person has discovered that it has actually happened, of course, he or she can decide what to do about it.

The push that causes one to "fall in love" at this level may be a bit of narcissism or dependency. Or it may be mostly physical chemistry—at least enough to raise the question of whether the phenomenon is more heat or love. Already at this point we are flirting with addiction, because love in this sense appears as an essentially choiceless phenomenon. The resulting loss of touch with a rational perspective, the emotional, impulsive responses, the obsessive thoughts that overwhelm the lover make him or her behave as one possessed. Addiction is not far off.

The second feature of romantic love is *passion*. Emotional circuits break down in the heat of passion: the entire focus of mind, soul, and body is on the beloved. There is no distraction, no diversion. Though we may find Dante's physiology quaint, we know what he means when he says that romantic love "moves the heart as the seat of spiritual emotion. It moves the brain as the center of perception. It moves the liver as the center of corporeal emotion."[2]

Romantic love, with its givenness and passion, has been around for a long time, but only recently has its relationship with addiction been considered.[3] As we have already noted, addiction is a word with strong overtones, often mistakenly linked exclusively to drugs like alcohol. But we have been arguing that addiction is best understood primarily as an *experience,* not as the body's metabolic reaction to the invasion of some chemical.

Recall the scenario of addiction as we try to relate this to a love story. Addiction is an intensifying experience which grows out of someone's habitual response to something that has special meaning to him or her. That behavior produces feelings of safety, reassurance, affirmation, even pleasure. It is our nature to repeat that which produces pleasure, affirmation, reassurance, and safety. As the addictive process grows in intensity, providing the desired result, we gradually lose our power to choose for or against the activity. Instead, we impulsively, even compulsively repeat the activity or return to the object of our affection. We don't have it anymore; it has us. As the old Chinese proverb reminds us: "The man takes a drink, the drink takes a drink, the drink takes the man."

We should stop talking only of drugs when we speak of addiction and look instead at the *self.* How do we acquire habits? How do those habits become dependencies? We live in a culture that feeds the addictive process by bombarding us with messages which suggest that we are inadequate, that we don't measure up, that "it's a jungle out there," and that we have to be prepared to pay any price to compete, to win, to succeed. All this is fertile ground for the addictive process to take root in. We come to rely on external bulwarks to protect us from the pain of stress. We turn to the fix, whether it is a drug, a date, or a deity.

But we have also been insisting that addiction is simply not an abnormality or an anomaly or an aberration; it only describes the nature of human existence. It is the destiny of life to maintain, secure, or discover a sense of authentic freedom, a sense of "I"-ness; but we too often find ourselves trapped in relationships and entangled in patterns of living that "leave us no choice."

The addict lacks the desire or confidence to come to grips with life on the strength of his or her own internal resources. The message: "Take care of me." The addict views life in a negative, cynical, almost paranoid light. The world around and the people in it are threats to his or her existence. The message: "Protect me."

The addict responds to stress by seeking quick relief. The message: "Sleep with me" or "Have a drink with me." The addict is less likely to be rebellious than frightened. The message: "Let me hide behind your strength"—whether it's the strength of a prayer group, the strength that comes from a lover, or the courage that comes out of a bottle.

The addict is generally passive and waits for things to happen. And when things don't happen in accordance with expectations, the response is frustration. The message: "Dominate me; decide for me, so that when something goes wrong I have somebody else to blame."

How does all this tie in with romantic love? Listen to the way the lyrics of popular romantic love songs put it: "I can't live . . . if living is without you." Or: "I need your love to survive. Without it I'm only half alive."

Standing back and reading those words literally, we're likely to say, "That's *sick*." But why is it sick?

D. H. Lawrence called it an *égoisme à deux*:[4] two people bonded together symbiotically, living off one another, each denying the other's individual right to exist independently. For all its dependency, addictive love is primarily a taking kind of love, an excessive and obsessive entanglement with the beloved, a compulsion to be bonded together forever—at the expense of other relationships, one's own development, and one's interests for the welfare of a community of other people.

A classic case is the heralded love story of F. Scott Fitzgerald and Sheilah Graham, which Stanton Peele cites in *Love and Addiction*. Once when she was to make a trip to New York, Fitzgerald countered, "You are looking for love, for someone to understand you. You have me. I love you and understand you. There's no need for you to go to New York."

Her obsession was equally breathtaking: "My living began when he arrived. . . . I looked into his face; searching it, trying to find its mystery, its wonder for me, and I said, almost prayerfully, 'If only I could walk into your eyes and close the lids behind me, and leave all the world outside.'"[5]

Erich Fromm minces no words in commenting on that kind of relationship: "If a person loves only one other person and is indifferent to the rest of his fellow human beings, love is no longer love but a symbiotic attachment of an enlarged egotism—a narcissistic sort of a monster."[6]

The usual reasons given to explain the epidemic rate of marriage breakup today include disputes over dual careers, problems with sex, tensions over money, and the all-purpose explanation of "irreconcilable differences." All are plausible. But they are all symptoms of the real culprit, namely, unrealistic expectations based on the addictive quality of the relationship during courtship. Marriage eventually resembles a case of burned-out addiction; spent, withdrawn, apathetic. Both partners are disillusioned that the other did not bring the expected happiness.

This addictive process begins innocently enough. A person falls in love. The good feeling produces a euphoric experience. The law that operates deep within us is that we will repeat or maintain whatever feels good to the psyche. We do this with such vigor and intensity that we barely notice that it is impossible to maintain that level of intensity. Then there is separation, withdrawal, a sense of depression: a recovery period that is climaxed by a reunion, and another round of intimacy which takes our lovers to still another depth.

This cycle repeats itself until the lovers finally reach their threshold of emotional tolerance and make the painful discovery that sentiment and passion do not make a relationship. The chemistry works temporarily. Each level in the process takes the lovers to new heights or depths of ecstasy. Soothe me; help me to escape to your world; help me survive; I need you; I am afraid without you; without you, I am only half alive; I am sick without you. . . .

Here is a letter purloined from the files of one passionate lover lost in an addictive relationship:

The days fly by but the moments seem to drag on and on. . . . I tell myself that it is only a few minutes of every day that I spend thinking of you when I know it is every hour.

To say that I miss you only trivializes the matter for me. I miss the "me" I become when there was "we." Now that there is no more "we" I am not "I" but only a shadow of my former self that became a self in you. Oh, I perform. I perform well. My routines are well accepted. You could even say that I have made a hit. But the hit that I make is a hit made by a hollow man; I am a man eroded by the experience of yesterday's love.

I would have, I could have lived my life without ever knowing you and not have missed the otherworldly experience of your love. But now that is only wishful thinking. Now that is over. And I am forever blessed (or cursed) by the memory of you.

And yet, and yet, the reality of my life does not erase the memory of your nearness. I have idealized you? I know. And in idealizing you, I miss the reality of you, me, us. I pray that you remember us but in your remembrance of us may the "you" of "us" go on to love again. Opportunity makes you free. Yet I selfishly hope that there is a part of you that is reserved only for "us."

I still feel that I cannot go on without the hope that there will be another "us"; perhaps that "us" will be realized in another. Can I live the pain again? Or will I? God, I want to be reconciled to myself. Come fill me again.

Is he lost in the relationship? Certainly, he *lost* the relationship. But is *he* lost? Yes and no. He seems willing to move ahead with his life. Yet he (1) writes the letter in the first place; (2) attempts to manipulate his beloved's feelings ("remember us," "reserve a spot for 'us'"); and (3) waffles in his decision to move ahead, still gripped by the fantasy that the relationship will resume. There is a poignant similarity here with an alcoholic in the early stages of a recovery process. Recovering alcoholics fantasize and dream about the day when they can return to the drug of their choice. They remember only the high times and choose to forget the hurtful consequences of their drinking career.

What are the consequences of an addictive love relationship?

● *A loss of choice and a forced dependency.* A fresh addiction is an affair with a new lover—inviting, exciting, delighting. It is always the rush of feeling, always the response, always the orgasm. A fresh addiction is a lover always waiting, always ready. It is the tormenting thrill of hearing your name whispered over and over. But as time passes, the addiction burns itself out, becoming a matter of going through the motions out of habit and need. An old addiction is a dry, joyless orgasm. An old addiction is settling last year's overdue bills, paying the tab for a good time that is over and can hardly be remembered, turning over the regular protection money to the extortioner just to avert the agony.

● *A narcissistic life-style.* My feelings go from being important to taking priority. Even the idea of sharing is perverted: the wino never offers someone else a swig from the bottle without a benumbed ulterior motive: "I'll probably need a fix from him sooner or later." In a romantic love addiction, it is *my* anxiety for love that must be served first. *Eros* reigns supreme.

● *A loss of "ego" or a loss of a sense of self.* The love letter quoted above expresses this eloquently. The writer had lost his identity in the relationship, and when the relationship ended, it was as if he was "over and out."

37

● *Disillusionment.* The loser in an addictive love relationship is like an embezzler, except that the currency is not money but life. There is the same deepening hole, the same need to cover tracks, the same impossibility of stopping. The odds of getting caught are even worse. We have remarked already that the person in an addictive emotional relationship feels as if there is only the one special person who can carry his or her burden. But with the deepening of this experience comes a gradual awareness that no one can in fact carry the burden of someone else's emotional needs. The sense of loss and anger can be overwhelming, because the lover counted on the beloved to always be there.

Not all love is addictive. There are criteria that can help us to distinguish authentic, give-and-take love from addictive love. Here are some of the questions lovers might ask themselves and each other (following Stanton Peele) to determine whether or not their relationship is endangered by addictive tendencies.

1. Does each of us have a secure belief in his or her own value? Could you, could I live without the other? Can both of us say: "I can make it on my own, but I would rather have you with me, I *choose* to have you with me?"

2. Are we improved by the relationship? Am I accomplishing more, am I getting stronger, am I developing my interpersonal skills?

3. Am I maintaining my serious interests and relationships outside of my primary relationship with you?

4. Is our relationship multidimensional? Do we have more going for us than just sex, for example, or a common interest in classical music or basketball or agro-engineering?

5. Are we friends as well as lovers?

6. Have we gotten beyond possessiveness and jealousy?

7. Do I celebrate your victories and personal growth—and you mine—or do these pose a threat to us?

8. Giving is the lifeblood of any relationship. Does each of us give for the sake of the other, or for the sake of a return on our investment?

9. Conversely, is each of us free to receive from the other? Or is either of us on a power trip that wants to control the giving and receiving?

10. Can I stand with you in your sorrows and triumphs without being swallowed up by them?

11. Do we dare to risk change and development in our relationship or in our family?

12. Is there space in our togetherness?[7]

Romantic love is here to stay. Despite the risks of addiction, that's a good thing, so long as the lovers seriously confront those dangers before acting on their feelings of falling headlong into a romantic journey to the stars. Unfortunately, many adults handle life's crisis points through a romantic "love affair." Depending on whose statistics you accept, as many as half of all men and women may be involved at some time or other in a romantic love relationship outside of their covenant of marriage. It seems to me that an affair outside of marriage is almost inevitably a case of addictive love. What are the dynamics of this particular kind of addictive love relationship?

The "affair" may be one consequence of a marriage that has been burned out by its own addictive patterns. After the flames of romance have burned down and the intoxicating highs of the relationship have given way to one long hangover, only the broken shell of a marriage relationship remains. Other relationships become more appealing. What do alcoholics do when sick to death from acute intoxication? They reach for another bottle—if possible one with a higher percentage of alcohol. Is that very different from the burned out and burned up spouse who hits the road in pursuit of a relational fix?

Let us further specify our examination of the dynamics of love and addiction in the romantic liaison outside marriage by looking at how they function in the life of a pastor (a profession whose casualty rate in this area is among the highest).

The fact is that pastors are often put upon by persons needing both physical and emotional intimacy. What is more, pastors often put themselves on other people out of a deep need for intimacy and caring. Some persons come to their pastor for counseling in integrity and innocence, requiring only assistance and insight to help solve a particular problem. Many others come out of a deep and more general need for intimacy and caring. The advice or message the pastor communicates will get across only if the conduit in which it is conveyed is care and acceptance.

It is at this point that fuses can be lit. If we who are pastors are particularly vulnerable to those same needs, we may find ourselves in a compromising position. In the terms we have been using in this book, we can get hooked on people. We become involved and lose our objectivity. Physical intimacy is the ultimate and often inevitable result. Too many pastors succumb to such circumstances, jeopardizing both their careers and their marriages. Too many more withdraw into lives of lonely isolation, unable or unwilling to share moments of intimacy. Incredibly, they find themselves emotionally involved with a person other than their spouse. The shame, the loneliness, and the fear work at cross purposes with the exhilarating experience of their new found intimacy.

Expressing moral or ethical disapproval of this by quoting Bible texts or pontificating about "professional ethics" may inflict more shame and fear, but these responses do not stem the tide. Today's permissive spirit and the easier access to personal relationships combine powerfully to make pastors more susceptible than in an earlier day to behavioral lapses that violate our values and standards of conduct. Yet that seems like a vapid rationalization that leads away from the truth of the matter.

To steel oneself against these feelings or to deny them or even to condemn ourselves for them is only a futile exercise in self-flagellation. We need to own our vulnerability, in a self-aware acceptance of our feelings.

Awareness of my own vulnerability is a painful thing. It helps to recognize that this is a part of my humanity regardless of the status of my marriage. In fact, the quality of the pastor's own married life is not necessarily a factor. A good marriage is no guarantee that the pastor is safe, nor do all unhappily married ministers have affairs. No male is naturally monogamous. At some level it is a struggle for every man to stay faithful to his spouse. (Unfortunately, women are beginning to rewrite the sociological givens and more of them seem now to surrender to the natural urge to "go with the flow" as well.) Coming to terms with that reality is a painful process for men in the ministry. Yet I find it a necessary, if gut-wrenching, mental process in a ministry of personal caring for and sharing with people, getting close, touching one another's spirits. Emotional intimacy is a risky but necessary element of authentic pastoral ministry.

I sometimes wish that John would have been more explicit in writing his gospel story of Jesus and the woman at the well. The dynamics for intimacy were there; the fuse was a fraction from being lit. The male pastor simply cannot be as confrontative with a woman as Jesus was in that encounter without simultaneously experiencing his own sexuality.

For a long time I felt alone on this matter, carefully keeping this vulnerability within me under wraps. Eventually, I dared to share my doubts and questions with a few trusted colleagues, fearing nevertheless that I might sound to them like a lecherous wolf in shepherd's clothing. Would I really only be stimulating the fire within me? Would I be seeking tacit permission to "go with" my feelings? Would I inadvertently be encouraging a weaker brother to give in to his vulnerability?

In fact, I discovered—thank God!—that I am not alone in this struggle. I have learned in a more profound way to thank God for who I am in Christ Jesus and to trust that God will complete the work he began in me.

Not that the risks have disappeared. Indeed I often wonder if our Puritan ancestors weren't right—at least partly—in practicing the "discipline of denial." Denial and self-denial, of course, are two different things. Self-denial, it seems to me, is a behavioral issue. Only in the strength of the Spirit of Jesus, and through the grace of his power am I able to overcome the impulse to gratify the desire of my weakened flesh. Denial is another matter. It is a pretense, a sham, a refusal to face reality squarely.

Were our Puritan ancestors partly right in carrying on the game: suppress the desire for intimacy and it will lose its spirit? Or are we in our own age of enlightenment partly right: give vent to some of those darker feelings from the shadow side of yourself and thus control them more effectively, more honestly? For that matter, must we always identify our passionate desire for intimacy with our shadowy flesh-infested self? Or may we claim this passion for intimacy as a part of our authentic self, to be owned, to be held up to God, and for which we can give him praise?

I raise these questions not so as to offer unambiguous answers to them, but as a hedge against this inquiry's becoming simply theoretical. When I write about the passions and vulnerability of pastors to addictive relationships, it is from the perspective not of some person "out there" but of the person within me. I invite the reader to be sensitive as well to that existentially vulnerable self in him, in her.

The servant role fits pastors especially well. After all, we are called to *serve*. It suits our need to be needed. If the phone does not ring for a day or two, if the calendar is not full, we feel anxious. Post-sermon, post-seminar, post-worship euphoria quickly dwindles down to a Monday morning "blah." From the heights to the depths. It's called withdrawal, and it isn't limited to drug addicts and pill-poppers. We become addicted to people, needing them around, needing them to rely on us, needing them to use us, to learn from us, needing their need for support and care. The "beeper" and the portable cordless telephone become the symbols of our indispensability.

To be hooked on people does not seem to be a negative addiction. But it can be a dangerous one, especially when our need narrows down to one special person who really seems to need us and whom we especially need, or when there is a space inside of us that needs filling when we are busy filling spaces for others.

Why does this addiction happen? Why do some drinking persons become alcoholics? Why do some of us fall prey to emotionally and/or physically intimate relationships outside of our own marriages? A delightful and perceptive fictional treatment of this issue is John Updike's novel *A Month of Sundays*. But like addiction to chemicals, it is difficult to explain *why* a person becomes addictive in relationships.

It is possible, however, to describe *how* it happens. And, Fritz Perls suggests, such awareness by and of itself can be curative.[8] If we are made aware of what we are doing, how we are behaving, what we are up to, we have before us the choice: to change or not to change behaviors.

How, then, does addiction get started? As it begins to feel good. Drinking feels good. We can preach and teach and threaten and warn our offspring to stay away from alcoholic beverages completely or to use them sparingly, but their experience that it feels good to be high will in many cases prevail over our sermons and lessons and the dire consequences we predict. A similar powerful influence of feeling good has an impact on helpers and healers. Pastors are the object of reactions that run the gamut from scathing criticism ("roast preacher" for Sunday dinner) to hero worship. Since much of the pastor's work, aside from Sunday worship, is carried out alone or with only one other person at a time, we can easily get the feeling that no one really knows the work we do. Except, perhaps, the lovely, lonely parishioner who by her eyes, her tone of voice, her touch, her dependency, tells you—perhaps without using the words—that you are really special. Naturally, that feels good. *And it is good!* But the problem is that it too easily sets up a pattern. It's the law within us. We tend to repeat that which makes us feel good.

The object of our attention and affection can be booze, caffeine, nicotine, relationships, even candy bars . . . whatever. The point is: if it did the job once, we assume it will do the job again. Our difficult responsibility is to decide whether something that makes us feel good *is* in fact good. The problem with intimate relationships is that they can dull our good sense and excite our craving for sensations in a much more subtle and "respectable" fashion than, say, alcohol does.

One of the critical factors is the affirmation we receive in our profession. It goes a little deeper than "feeling good." With good reason, we are quite emphatic when pointing out how sick an addicted person is. It is insane for a person to return to an involvement which causes pain, whether it be abuse of alcohol or pills or food. Yet somehow the person gathers a few grains of self-affirmation from the object of addiction. It enables him or her to feel not only good but also powerful or competent or in control or loved. Intimate relationships in our professions can do that to us—make us feel we are loved, make us feel free, alive, fresh, and forever young. Another law within us. One way or another, we *will* get self-affirmation.

Often we get the self-affirmation we crave in the context of our working world instead of our "at home" world. It is there that our self-esteem is won or lost. Our evaluation of who we are is tied to what we make of ourselves in our career, how much control we can muster over the immediate environment, how much money we can make. There are many mountains to climb, many prizes to be won, so we invest more of ourselves there. At home by contrast we may be ignored or taken for granted. There are no promotions there, no measurable goals to achieve, few strokes to receive. So we invest less there.

Expectations that are laid on us early in life—to strive, to be strong, to succeed—are later internalized and intensified. The stake is our self-esteem. And in our professional life, where we are struggling to make it, we are most attractive and vulnerable to a romantic liaison. Fundamentally, what we want is to be loved and accepted and affirmed and stroked. We get a measure of that at work, but barely a grain at home. And so we lose touch with our emotional investment at home, and we cut ourselves off emotionally from the primary relationships there. Success, the value we have internalized, becomes the way to get love. Whatever creative spirit, whatever thoughtful moments, whatever magical insights, whatever well-spring of emotional life we have are all expressed in vocation. Home becomes a vacuum. There is pressure but no spirit, no room to breathe.

Professional success and the affirmation that goes with it make us vulnerable to opportunities for addictive relationships in the world of our work. The pattern is familiar. A feeling of freedom washes over us, putting off our consciousness of growing old. From our perch sitting on top of the world, we feel in control. Our prospects seem unlimited. We lead with our strengths, the very qualities that attract and seek. And at first we are rewarded.

As with all addictions, however, the returns diminish. Affection turns into obsession, and the highs are no longer high enough. Our pursuit of them becomes more frantic, and our sense of perspective, once so broad and boundless, narrows into tunnel vision. Freedom turns into an albatross of compulsion around our neck. The reality of the aging process seeps back into our consciousness. Other relationships fade into painful insignificance, even as the relationship that is the object of our addiction evolves into something hostile-dependent (like the junkie who is repulsed by drugs). Shame becomes our constant companion. The drive for success, which was a big factor in getting us here in the first place, is sacrificed at the altar of the relationship.

What do we get from the addictive intimate relationship itself? What is the payoff that drives us to continue something that, on any rational calculation, is contrary to our own interests? It goes deeper than just feeling good or being affirmed in our sexuality. An illuminating parallel is the beverage alcohol addict, for whom—believe it or not—the payoff is often the experience of rejection. If I drink myself out of spouse, job, and church, no one will bother me and I can do what I want—and get what I deserve—no pressure, no hassle. For those of us whose only contact with Skid Row is when we drive through in the security of our cars, it seems like a stage where countless individual tragedies are moving toward their unhappy endings. But Skid Row is not perceived that way by many of its residents. They know that they may be killed in an assault, or die from an overdose, exposure, or seizures. But they won't die from stress. Benumbed to the anxiety of guilt, they succeed at repulsion, for as long as the binge lasts.

So what is the payoff in the intimate addictive relationship? Consider the person who becomes involved in such a relationship with the pastor of a successful church or a leader in a community. Consider how she perceives him: as an authority figure, as a representative of God, someone potent and dominant. This is the definite turn-on for both parties. Not a few ministers secretly harbor authority-messiah complexes, which occasionally surface when they use expressions like "*my* church" or "*my* people" to speak of the congregation they pastor or "*my* patient" for someone they are counseling. It may be reflected in the attitude that the rise and fall of the church or the recovery of the person is on the pastor's shoulders. If we are moved by that dynamic, it is altogether too easy for an encounter with one of "our people" or "our patients" to become an intimate involvement. For relief purposes only!

Our own personality makeup plays a role here too. All of us are, more or less, stimulus-seekers or stimulus-receivers, seducible or seductive. Addicts are high-flying, high-living stimulus-seekers. Recall here, too, our discussion in the previous chapter of freedom's paradox and the denial of death. Helping and healing seem to offer us more than the simple satisfaction of doing well. It can often be a high. The withdrawal symptoms pastors can experience following the intensity of climactic breakthrough therapy are not simple fatigue. So they need to be aware of the stimulus received or the stimulus sought in their relationships with their clientele. And of the consequent withdrawal.

Withdrawal. Relationships always end. There is pain in letting go or giving up the relationship. Some evidence suggests that beverage alcohol addicts need twelve to eighteen months to withdraw emotionally from their active addiction, and after that they must practice a program that continually reaffirms their sobriety. Something similar applies to relationships that have become addictive. Sheldon Van Auken's description in *A Severe Mercy* of his relationship with his beloved Davy sounds enviable until he walks the reader through the painful account of his own traumatic withdrawal on being cut off from her.[9]

What can be done?

We earlier cited Fritz Perls's suggestion that simple awareness of the dangers may be curative. From a strictly humanistic perspective, not taking into consideration God's present involvement in the world, we have it in us to make a better self and a better world. But without disregarding our own inner resources here, we need more than awareness. We need the power of grace. There are several specific things we can do, however, to give this grace a better chance of working.

First, pastors themselves need supervision—and not just in emergency situations of crisis intervention. We need to talk regularly to another professional about our ministry. We need feedback. If a male therapist is seeing a woman in counseling for more than four sessions, he needs help with that encounter. Too often we discount or avoid peer supervision partly because—as one pastor suggested to me, "we tend to be competitors rather than cooperators." He expressed his own gratitude to be a part of a prayer and share group. Pastors do need consultation— especially in the delicate matter of vulnerability to intimacy outside of marriage. Is this something we "simply haven't gotten around to" because we are already in the early stages of an addiction?

Second, since external resources for internal gratification constitute a major dynamic in addiction, it is helpful honestly to examine the extent to which our good feelings about ourselves depend solely on persons, things, relationships outside of ourselves. The familiar refrain of the unfaithful husband—that "the other woman" understands him better than his wife does— manifests an addictive dynamic. Whether the "other woman" understands me or not is really beside the point. The critical question is "Do *I* understand me?" The mystery of Christ in us is relevant in this connection. To know and experience the indwelling of Christ can be a vital resource for preventing a sick dependency on involvements outside of ourselves.

Third, while quoting Bible texts is not an adequate way to cope with our susceptibility to addictive relations, focusing on the sexuality of Jesus can be helpful. Without a doubt, Jesus was sexually integrated in a healthful way. Besides, he was an attractive person, and one who drew not just crowds but persons crying out for intimacy. The women in his life felt close to him. They leaned on him: his mother, the Syrophoenician woman, the woman from Bethany, Mary Magdalene, Martha, the woman at the well. All of these relationships were potentially addictive. The feeling Mary Magdalene was expressing to the risen Jesus outside the empty tomb, to which he responded "Don't cling to me"—or more literally, "Touch me no more"—is freighted with natural human emotions. The song "I Don't Know How to Love Him," from *Jesus Christ Superstar,* probably conveys accurately the feelings that many women had for Jesus. But he was able to love these persons in an intimate manner without succumbing to an addictive or physical relationship. Can we learn to pray for the strength to strive to emulate the sexuality of Jesus as part of our ongoing attempt to be like him?

Fourth, our relationship with our spouse is a key factor in coping with other relationships that confront us. Unless we are willing to see this relationship as a priority that takes precedence *before* our ministry, we will find it difficult if not finally impossible to maintain our sensual equilibrium and pastoral propriety.

In the end we must be prepared simply to surrender who we are to God. That's neither a pious cliché nor a shrug of the shoulders that leaves our flesh up for grabs. Rather, it is a very intentional and painful spiritual discipline in which we lay who we are at God's feet, in effect saying, "Lord, here I am: this is how I am. Take me, take all of me. I can't handle it myself." Internal obedience on this matter can never be just the consequence of a herculean exertion of our willpower. Do the legwork, yes. Pay your behavioral dues and know when to go home. But own the internal reality and then give it to God.

This chapter, like the next two, concludes with a case study in which the chapter's inevitably theoretical discussion of a struggle against addiction is given a more personal human dimension. Readers should bear in mind that these case studies are intended as a device to stimulate further reflection (there are some questions at the end of each); they are not stories cooked up to prove that if a counselor follows the insights set forth in the chapter success will automatically follow.

There are no moral surprises that catch us unawares. As Paul suggests in Romans 1, the truth of who we are and what we ought to do is largely self-evident. The moral law in regard to adultery, for example, only confirms what we innately know, all rationalistic meanderings aside. That doesn't take away from the existential struggle to do and to be what we know we *ought* to do and be. To "walk the talk" of fidelity may be a simple matter; it isn't an easy one. Ask Jim Sloan. Ask Pastor Rule.

CASE STUDY

The End of the Affair

Pastor Bob Rule reflected on what approach to take with his friend and parishioner Jim Sloan. It had been a month since Jim had been receiving counsel from Pastor Bob; and there had been little change in Jim's feelings, behavior, or conflict. He was emotionally and physically involved with Mary Fremont. Today he had disclosed the full extent of this relationship to his pastor.

The seeds of this problem were planted at least two years earlier. Jim had been transferred by his company to Omaha, Nebraska, to a new office and a new responsibility. The firm was a national insurance carrier and Jim was a rising young executive. He and his wife, Sarah, with their four children had moved every three or four years. Each move represented a promotion for Jim but was a traumatic event for Sarah. She often complained, "Each time I get settled and make new friends, we have to move again. I'm tired of this, and it's hard on the children. I wish you would consider our feelings more often."

Jim's response was usually a frustrated, "What can I do? Are you willing to give up your financial security and life-style? Do you want to do without the things we have now?"

The issue wasn't being resolved and the tension in the Sloan family grew. So did the distance between Jim and Sarah. Eventually they each began to retreat and withdraw from one another. Sarah found some solace in her Bible study fellowship group. Jim kept busy in his effort to "get to the top."

Each was vulnerable to their needs for intimacy and affection, needs not being met at home. After about a year in Omaha, Jim began to develop a friendly relationship with one of his co-workers, also an executive with the firm. He and Mary Fremont began their friendship with casual lunch, then a drink together after work, then a business trip together, and finally sexual encounter. It was about four months from that first lunch to the first sexual encounter. Their shared professional interests, together with a mutual commitmentlessness to one another, seemed to provide access for an easy and intimate relationship. This was compounded by Jim's frustration with Sarah, who became increasingly wary, distant, and now suspicious: "You're not getting it at home. Where are you getting it?"

Pastor Rule became involved in the Sloans' problems when Sarah began to seek his counsel. Lonely and fearful, she saw her relationship with Jim deteriorating. He was away from home during the evening more frequently. She complained: "He doesn't seem to care about our family anymore. We used to be able to enjoy one another when the kids went to bed. Now all he wants to do when he is home is read and be left alone. I'm afraid that I'm losing him."

Sarah's emotional stress led Pastor Rule to suspect that something more was amiss in Jim's life than simple loss of interest in his marriage. He made a point of seeing Jim privately. Jim was a person of fairly traditional values, who held religion, the "Protestant work ethic," family devotion and loyalty in high esteem. He was fearful of the opportunity Pastor Rule's intervention afforded him, but also a little relieved.

After several weeks of discussing job pressures and what he termed a "nagging and meddlesome wife," Jim shared with the pastor what had been going on in his life for the past year. "Mary seems to understand and accept me. I feel so free with her. For the first time in my life, it feels like I can be myself. When I am with Mary, I feel I can breathe again. I can cry; I can laugh; I feel young again. Sarah and I have been married for twelve years now and it's—well, a drag. The same old hassles about moving so often. Sarah doesn't give me any support. With Mary I feel like I am talking with an equal, not just dragging someone along.

"Pastor, I love her and I need her. I just don't know what to do. I know what the Bible says; I know the position of the church. I know that what I'm doing is wrong. Don't think that doesn't matter to me; it does. I know I violate my family, my God, and my values. I don't want to lose Mary. And I don't want to lose my family, but I need to take care of *me,* too. What should I do, Pastor?"

Pastor Rule responded by turning the question back to Jim: "What do you want to do and what should you do?"

Jim shook his head and began to weep. "I know what I *should* do. I should leave Mary and return to my wife. Probably we should get counseling. But I can't. Don't you see? I feel so, so human, so alive when I am with Mary. She gives me a reason for living. It sounds dumb, but it's true."

Pastor Rule informed Jim that Sarah probably suspected his unfaithfulness to her. He suggested that Jim confront the matter and be open with his wife. "Perhaps," said Pastor Rule, "it could mean the turning point in your relationship with your wife."

Jim responded, "But I'm not ready for that. It would hurt Sarah too much. Besides, I can't jeopardize my relationship with Mary. I won't give that up."

The conversation had gone on for about an hour and a half. At one point Jim defended his position by stating in an almost angry tone of voice, "Sometimes we go to church together, and I have never felt so near to God as when I sit in church holding Mary's hand. She makes me feel high on life."

Questions for Further Reflection:

1. What counsel would you offer Mary Fremont? Is she, like Jim, a victim of self-defeating behavior?

2. How do you feel about the morality of the phrase "Go where the love is?" Is it good advice?

3. Does Pastor Rule have a trump card in the official discipline and admonition of the church? If so, should he play it?

4. With whom do you identify in this case? How? Why?

5. Comment on the judgment: "Jim Sloan is a self-serving narcissist."

6. It is sometimes said that "every good marriage can sustain a

romantic affair on the part of one or both partners." Comment.

7. Where does addiction come to play in the dynamics of Jim's behavior? Is his powerlessness a factor? Does that make a difference in how you would help him? or confront him? or discipline him?

CHAPTER **IV**

Alcohol and Addiction

When God confronted Adam in the Garden of Eden and asked him whether his recognition and shame that he was naked had anything to do with eating the fruit of the forbidden tree, Adam had his excuse ready: "It's that woman you gave me. . . . "

Such a response is called *projection.* It's a tactic we're all acquainted with. We'd like to explain our problems and pathologies in terms of forces, powers, or other people outside of ourselves, things over which we have no control.

The readiness to project responsibility elsewhere is familiar in cases of addiction to alcohol. In an article on "The Human Side of Addiction," social psychologist Stanton Peele links contemporary attitudes toward alcoholism with our readiness to reject accountability for our difficulties and to try to eliminate the anxiety that comes from being responsible for their causes and remedies.[1] Self-reflection can be painful, so we usually avoid it if possible.

In the past several years, it has become common for professionals in the field to view alcoholism as an uncontrollable disease with mysterious chemical or genetic origins. Alcoholics, it is said, are born, not made; there are people who are biochemically predisposed to use alcohol addictively from birth to death.

Peele identifies several factors that make the idea of alcoholism as a disease attractive:

- It is appealing as a description of the experiences of many people who find themselves inexorably drawn toward intoxication from the first drink they took.

- It enables people to relieve false guilt by offering a biological explanation for something that might otherwise be regarded as moral failure.

- It is supported by powerful forces within the drug and alcohol establishment, including the American Medical Association, the World Health Organization, the National Council on Alcoholism, and Alcoholics Anonymous.

- It feeds our hunger for clear-cut medical solutions for complex problems.[2]

By comparison with the old image of alcoholics as despicable degenerates fit only for the soup line until they finally drink themselves to death, the disease theory is certainly more humane. The goal of releasing the addict from an overwhelming sense of guilt while at the same time educating the public to see suffering alcoholics as people who need to be helped, not condemned, is certainly admirable.

Furthermore, recent research has led scientists to link genetic and biochemical factors to the disease theory. In Denmark in the 1970s, Dr. Donald Goodwin conducted genetic studies of some five thousand children of alcoholic parents, who were adopted into nonalcoholic homes. He found the incidence of alcoholism to be four times greater than he expected.[3] While it is true that we cannot locate the defective chromosome under the microscope, there seems to be definite indications that a hereditary factor is involved. Alcoholism in one's family is almost the only reliable indicator of whether a person could become an alcoholic.

In addition to these hereditary factors are biochemical factors—how the body's chemicals react to alcohol in its system. The main pathway of metabolism of alcohol is the same for alcoholics and nonalcoholics. Alcohol, taken orally, is absorbed from the stomach and intestines and carried in the blood throughout the body. It is then broken down by liver enzymes into acetaldehyde, which in turn is broken down into acetate and then to carbon dioxide and water and excreted from the body. Acetaldehyde is a very toxic substance, believed to be what causes the damage to the liver, heart muscle, and brain cells.

Researchers have found that, in alcoholics, some of the acetaldehyde goes to the brain, where it interacts with the amines to form a new class of compounds called isoquinolines. One of these, formed from acetaldehyde and dopamine, is known as tetrahydroisoquinoline, or TIQ.

Dr. Virginia Davis, of Houston, first discovered TIQ in brains of alcoholics while she was researching brain cancer. She performed her research on brains of Skid Row drunks who had died, and was surprised to find TIQ, which she knew was a product of heroin breakdown. TIQ, then, is thought to cause the addiction in alcoholics; that is, to cause their physical compulsion to drink beverage alcohol.[4]

In 1977, Drs. Myers and Melchio at Purdue University did a very interesting experiment in which they injected small amounts of TIQ into the brains of rats that had previously refused alcohol. Following the injection the rats drank alcoholically. They became intoxicated, stumbled, fell, and experienced tremors and convulsions on withdrawal. Even after several months without alcohol and without further injections, the rats still preferred alcohol to water.[5]

It would appear, then, that an inherited factor causes an alcoholic to metabolize alcohol differently, forming increased amounts of acetaldehyde, some of which goes to the brain and reacts with dopamine to form TIQ, which in turn causes the addiction to alcohol.

The disease theory is certainly one aspect of a multidimensional human problem. But when we emphasize this theory, and define dependency on drugs like heroin and beverage alcohol in terms of a characteristic of the drug ("addictive") rather than the person ("addictable"), we diminish the truth about alcohol addiction. We tend to place responsibility for the addiction on the drug and responsibility for recovery ultimately on health care people instead of on the alcoholic himself.

Addiction is first of all a life-style, a behavioral disorder. Alcohol abuse is a learned behavior cultivated by a habitual readiness to take to drink whenever a painful situation arises. Both research data and my own pastoral experience confirm this judgment. Addiction is a way of coping with reality. Sobell, Sobell, and Pattison document this contention with over eighty studies in which they found that controlled drinking was possible for some alcoholics.[6]

There is no question that alcohol, heroin, and other drugs have a powerful debilitating effect on body tissues. But this physical reality does not in itself cause or indicate addiction. I am inclined to view the notion of "physical addiction" as incomplete at best, most probably questionable.

Alcoholism is not physically contagious. Being with a drunk may sicken me, but it won't make me drunk unless I choose to drink with him too long. Nor does the frequent comparison of alcoholism with diabetes support a disease theory: diabetics can point to their malfunctioning pancreas, but alcoholics can identify no comparably diseased organ in their bodies—except, perhaps facetiously, their brain, where judgments are made.

Cellular changes certainly do take place in the alcoholic's body. Consequently, detoxification is a real and often painful necessity. But painful physical craving is present only during the detoxification period. Thereafter, there is no evidence of physical addiction, though of course some of the consequences of alcohol abuse on the body may remain—liver or brain damage, dehydration, malnutrition, damage to the central nervous system, or heart disease. But if these complications indicate alcohol abuse, they are not in themselves indisputable evidence of continued addiction.

Traditional theories of alcoholism as a disease also appeal to cellular adaptivity as evidence. Because continual abuse of alcohol—and other depressants—weakens cellular structure in the body, the tolerance-withdrawal-craving cycle is reactivated with much more intensity if an alcoholic returns to the drug after a long period of abstinence. A typical Skid Row chronic alcoholic will get drunk and physically sick on a half pint of cheap wine because of this diminished tolerance. The cellular structure can no longer adapt to the drug.

The disease conceptualists report consistently that alcoholics who return to drinking after sustained abstinence suffer grossly exaggerated physical and psychological symptoms. Their bodies and minds react as if they had never been off the drug. Withdrawal symptoms become as chronic as the physical craving. What causes this has not been explained. But this experience of the chronic alcoholic does not prove that his or her alcoholism is a disease. It fails to explain *why* the person returned to beverage alcohol after the drug was out of his or her system. The disease concept is not sufficient to explain alcoholism. It represents only a corner of this complex addiction.

Consider a more commonsense approach to understanding alcoholism. Most people have seen an "Are You An Alcoholic?" questionnaire. The typical questions are: Do you gulp? Do you "sneak" drinks? Do you drink alone? Are you comfortable in a group only after a few drinks? "Yes" answers are supposed to be indicators of alcoholism, but in fact they are pointers to a variety of alcohol problems. Alcoholism is not a monolithic problem with one chemical source.

Some persons ruin their lives or invariably get into legal hassles with booze. Others rely on it only under certain circumstances. Some steadily increase their intake over the years; others drink violently but periodically. These might better be considered examples, not of alcoholism, but of alcoholism*s*.

Addiction has to do with the effect a drug produces on a given person. Generally this is an effect that relieves tension; but paradoxically it decreases one's ability to cope with life's complexities, thus causing more anxiety, not less. Persons who are addicted to a drug are addicted to the experience that the drug creates for them. The depressing effects of beverage alcohol lessen a person's feelings of pain and sense of life's difficulties at the same time than they cause the person to deal less capably with those difficulties. Potential addicts who turn to booze in order to gain rewards they are not presently earning or receiving from life will eventually find that their only rewards come exclusively from the drug experience itself. And so the merry-go-round of addiction proceeds.

I believe the disease theory of alcoholism serves a purpose. The medical profession now recognizes that alcoholics need treatment. Public drunkenness is being decriminalized in most states. Alcoholics Anonymous is now accepted as a creditable organization and alcoholics and their families are being helped.

Let us now get on to the business of treating alcoholics and their families more effectively and from a more complete perspective. If we recognize alcoholism as a behavioral disorder, it will be much simpler to implement the necessary treatment modalities: early intervention, strong confrontation, tough love, and a radical, spiritually based program of living.

Effective treatment of alcoholism does not necessitate the typical medical model approach. And historically alcoholics have not successfully sustained treatment from the medical perspective—or, for that matter, from the psychiatric or religious perspectives. One treatment modality, however, does stand out as being effective: the program and fellowship of Alcoholics Anonymous, which teaches in summary:

1. I can't.
2. God can.
3. I believe I'll let him.

To understand any individual case of addiction to a drug, we must ask, "What does this person derive from the drug and from experiencing its effect?" Note the difference between this question for understanding an addiction problem and the more conventional and traditional procedures to identify an addiction problem: How often does the person drink? How often is he drunk? When does he begin drinking during the day? Does he drink alone? Does he act out antisocially when he drinks? These criteria may not detect an addiction problem until long after the person is readily amenable to an effective recovery modality.

The question, "What does 'boozing or using' do for the person?" will inevitably elicit answers like these: It fills time; structures life; provides a reassuring ritual; grants power; grants sexual potency and/or freedom; facilitates a positive identity; alleviates anxiety; provides the ingredients for successful socialization. If we begin asking this question, "What does boozing and using do for you?" we may pick up an addiction problem much earlier in the cycle, perhaps before it even appears as a problem to any but those closest to the individual.

A crucial factor for many people who resort to depressant drugs is the drive for power and achievement. North American culture places a high premium on the ability to control or manage one's environment. High on the list of truths we believe to be self-evident is this one: that with enough willpower, enough charm, enough human potential, enough political machismo, enough muscle, enough brain power, I can say to that mountain, "Be cast into the sea" and it will be done . . . and if the mountain stands firm it's because of my personal weakness. This success-oriented life-style is social Darwinism—the "survival of the fittest" *ethos.* The weak and disabled and underprivileged are sifted in this sieve; and if you can't hold your own, it's just too bad.

The addict may be one of those persons who has been sifted through the sieve but refuses to tolerate the frustrating experience of failure and limitation. So he or she drinks or takes drugs, compulsively, to forget failure, to flee fear, to run from rejection. The resulting deterioration of body and mind increases the person's inadequacy for meeting personal goals—and increases the dependency. Those who have bought into the "Protestant work ethic" will experience guilt feelings for failing to get done what should be getting done. More drinking . . . and the beat goes on—a vicious descending spiral.

Because individual accomplishment is cultivated in our culture, many people experience a failure as evidence of inadequacy and come to feel trapped by their feelings of inadequacy. Drinking or drug-taking is one way of responding.

In this respect, the addiction experience—as we shall see in more detail in the next chapter—is not unlike the religious "high" that characterizes some people in evangelical Christian circles. In the protective custody, whether of spirits or *spiritus,* all pain and anxiety are removed—for a time. The world seems to become manageable. It *feels good* to be "high," chemically or religiously. Philosopher Arthur Holmes has put his finger squarely on the danger in this:

> Personal, private, feelingful experience, in fact, is not what life is all about; it is the reality and truth of things that counts. Experience is not what Christianity is primarily about: it, too, is concerned with the reality and truth of things. . . . Experiences can be induced by hypnosis, created by fantasy, duplicated by hallucinatory drugs. . . . Experience is a shifting sand. And to focus on having an experience can become egocentric and hedonistic— and that is not what evangelical Christianity is all about.[7]

Holmes continues, "Authentic Christianity is about the reality of God and our place in his creation." *Our place* in creation. We are contingent and finite beings who are born in need of a Savior, a power greater than ourselves to sanctify and satisfy.

That's a truth which isn't too palatable among a people who may still confess with their mouths that Jesus is Lord, but whose life-style depicts an attempt to lord it over their own lives as well as the lives of others.

There is a *macho* dimension to much alcohol abuse: drinking, even to the point of intoxication, is associated with masculinity and power. Who is it that hustles beer on television? Athletes. And adolescent boys take a cue, not from the sports star's athletic ability, but from his glamorized drinking. There's no doubt that a key aspect of the experience of alcohol is the illusion of power it offers, the feeling of potency. That this is a temporary illusion at best is laughably but pitiably illustrated by the gap between how sexually aroused a drunk can feel and how sexually impotent he really is when intoxicated.

This kind of alcohol abuse, I contend, is running rampant among people whom we would never think of as "having a drinking problem." Exaggeration? Hardly! For every obvious addict among us, there are at least ten others whose drinking and pilling is an effort to fill the inadequacy, inferiority, and impotency gaps in their lives. Sadly, the power of the gospel is also foolishness to those who have discovered the power of Jim Beam, Jack Daniels, and the rest of the boys in the barrel.

We have said that addiction is better understood with reference to the person using the chemical rather than the substance itself, because addiction is primarily to an experience. Addiction is not the exclusive property of a drug but a personality characteristic, and the boundaries of addiction are not marked off by drugs alone. There are parallels in areas of human behavior other than compulsive drug use.

Certainly, psychoactive drugs have a direct and sometimes disastrous impact on those who take them. Their effect on conscious awareness and feelings are immediate. Three martinis at lunch can kill the pain or raise your hopes or make Gloria the waitress look extremely attractive—all for the price of $4.50. But there are many other involvements and activities that provide some persons the kind of experience which leads to addiction— gambling, overeating, overtreatment, overwork or overplaying, television watching or hyper-religiosity. All of these can be regarded as and dealt with as addictions.

What is the addicting element that these activities share with drinking? All offer the chance for an all-consuming sensation that minimizes the conscious and painful awareness of life's limitations and freedom's tenuousness. What turns any activity into an addiction is centered in the person who is overcome by it. Personality, situation in life, motivation—all can work together in producing addictive behavior in a person.

If a person turns to sitting at the dinner table or the desk, standing at the bar or the roulette wheel, to escape psychic or physical pain; resorts to this increasingly for relief; experiences relief when engaged in it; feels anxiety and guilt when deprived of it; then that person will become addicted.

Heroin addicts, for example, are known to grow out of the habit when they can substitute methadone for heroin or when they can form a dependency on an institution such as a hospital or prison. It is the act and style of dependency to which addicts are addicted—it is that which "turns them on." The shift in the object of addiction from heroin to methadone to the institution is only incidental.[8]

Behind the astonishing success of bizarre religious cults that are able to brainwash teenagers and young adults lies a totally controlled and dependency-facilitating environment. Uncertainty and anxiety are submerged under the worship of the cult leaders. Identification with the cult's total way of life dissolves all personal aim and/or ambition to be a self-actualizing person.

But if addiction can appear in *any* type of repeatable involvement, with the activity or substance becoming addictive or not according to internal factors in the one using the substance or practicing the activity, can we recognize when addiction exists? Some characteristics can serve as criteria for addiction. Among them are the following:

• First a word of caution. Addiction is a **continuum.** Very rarely is a person's whole life dedicated completely to an addiction, as seen, for example, in the Skid Row alcoholic. The population of Skid Row represents only 3 percent of addicted alcoholics. The other 97 percent retain more or less—to outward appearances—their ordinary circumstances of life. But they are on a continuum of which it can be said that alcohol controls their lives to a significant extent. Persons are more or less addicted, depending on how much their habits control their lives.

• An addiction can **consume** a person and **distract** him or her from all other involvements. As we illustrated in the last chapter with the romantic love affair, the object of affection becomes the object of obsession. This is harmful because it diminishes the person and undercuts his or her life.

• Addiction is **not a pleasurable experience.** The object of obsession becomes the answer to and then the root of fear, anxiety, and guilt. The occasion for using is not one of pleasure but of pain. The mood set is not easy and light but difficult and heavy.

• Addiction is signalled by an **inability to choose not to do** something. Can the person sometimes turn away from the involvement in a situation which ordinarily calls for it? If so, he or she is not addicted.

The point that addiction can cover many involvements does not take away from the fact that alcoholism remains the #1 addiction in terms of lives lost, families destroyed, dollars wasted, accidents caused, and physical, psychological, and social problems incurred. Among the addictions of many kinds, shapes, and sizes that plague people we know and love, the various kinds of alcoholisms represent a significantly tragic category.

By contrast, nonaddictive behavior implies that the person knows when to stop doing something because it is harmful or detrimental to his or her life or to another person's life. People who have enough quality sources of satisfaction in life will not be so vulnerable to putting all their eggs in one basket, psychologically, spiritually, or socially. We will be less inclined to suppose that one substance or activity or relationship alone can bring us contentment—less inclined, in other words, to an addictive life-style—if we are gaining sufficient satisfaction from personal relationships with others.

People who have a positive self-image will not consciously hurt themselves by becoming enslaved to any one activity or substance. A healthy respect for oneself implies an unwillingness to become a person out of control, subject to outside forces that are foreign and destructive. Nonaddicts will have a healthy measure of self-acceptance to cope with the wolves of guilt and anxiety at the door.

A profound theological insight into nonaddictive behavior emerges from the first answer in the Heidelberg Catechism, which makes it clear that being a Christian does not mean being *obsessed* with Jesus Christ, but being focused by him and directed by him to be obedient to him in every area of life. My only comfort in life and death, the Catechism says, is not simply knowing "that I belong to my faithful Savior Jesus Christ" but also being willing and ready by the power of his Spirit, to live for him in whatever I do.

The nonaddicted person is not exempt from or immune to the lure of addictive behaviors. But he or she is able to acknowledge and face the problem in order to begin dealing effectively with it.

Is it worthwhile to describe such characteristics of a well-integrated person and propose some suggestions for helping people to get there? In particular, what does this ideal-sounding model of a well-integrated person have to do with the massive suffering and personal breakdown associated with alcoholism? Those are legitimate questions. There are some people who would claim that the only realistic way to confront alcoholism is via the surefire prevention that total abstinence alone makes possible. I disagree. For one thing, legislating abstinence as a norm is simply not biblical. But more to the point from our perspective in this book, abstinence is tangential to the source of the problem. We must address the issue of prevention from the broader base offered by a description of a well-integrated person and of how we can help to make that a reality in a particular individual.

This is not a matter of gimmicks—or, to use a more respectable term, "techniques." There are "how to" books and cassettes and workshops aplenty, each with its own set of slick, sleek, simplistic answers. Alas, the glib "tricks of the trade" we learn at seminars tend to flop when we try them out at home. With good reason we are disillusioned by and suspicious of surefire simple solutions to complicated people problems. The paragraphs that follow are not intended as a clear and final answer to the question, "What makes a person healthy or nonaddictive, and how do we help him or her to get there?" I can only offer some suggestions which may in turn stimulate further creative response on the reader's part.

First, I am increasingly convinced of the importance of the church and its program as the locus for developing well-integrated persons. Some people might propose other candidates for this role—the family, or health-care institutions, or Christian organizations outside the church. But on its own, the family tends to fragment its members (two out of three homes are in trouble interpersonally). Health-care systems tend to be ineffective without an interface with the message of the church. "Parachurch" religious organizations may offer a positive intervention tool, but unless this gift becomes part of the church community's program and focus, it is likely to be a short-lived "high" at best. I believe the maturity and full measure of perfection found in Christ (Ephesians 4:13) can blossom and bear fruit only when we are rooted in his body.

Second, having said that, we must add immediately that pastors alone cannot make the church into this kind of community. Nor is it enough to rely on a corps of volunteers, despite the importance of involving lay persons in the ministry of the congregation. A voluntary staff is beautiful, but temporary. A paid, professional staff accountable to the pastor is no longer a luxury for a church that intends seriously to face its responsibility to be the locus of inter- and intrapersonal growth "toward the full measure of perfection in Christ."

A major frustration felt by ministers today is the direct and clear exposure they have to the gaps, the addictions, the *anomie* of the members of their congregation, the fragmented families, the apathetic teenagers, the complacent aristocrats and secularists—and a feeling of the powerlessness of attempts to intervene effectively. The pulpit often becomes the place to ventilate that frustration. In order to get beyond railing at the "evil times" in which we live, I would encourage churches and pastors to marshall the necessary resources and appoint the staff needed to make intervention programs a central part of the church's life and ministry instead of an annual special event geared to give people a spiritual shot in the arm.

A third suggestion has to do with the content of "wholeness." What do whole people within the family of God look like? Can we identify some characteristics demonstrated by whole persons who express their maturity in Christ? Recalling that these comments are intended as suggestive rather than hard and fast rules, let us consider a few characteristics which might provide helpful pointers to such wholeness:

• *A balanced perspective.* Whole persons enjoy their bodies, minds, and spirits, exercising themselves in these areas in a balanced manner. Above and beyond his role in the history of salvation, David (though by no means untouched by sin's effects) is an exemplary biblical model of balance. The picture we have of him in the Old Testament is of one who enjoyed living and giving expression to the full range of his abilities, physically, spiritually, and emotionally. He was a healthy person, and God certainly enjoyed this special son.

• *Flexibility.* Or, to put it in the contemporary colloquialism: "going with the flow." Whole persons can tolerate frustrated goals without losing hope or cool. They adjust, change direction, compromise where appropriate. The apostle Paul's strength surely lay here. More than one missionary journey was interrupted. Frustrated by numerous obstacles and the unspecified "thorn in the flesh," he learned to remain content through it all.

• *Focus.* Whole persons have a purpose in life. To borrow a phrase from Frankl, they are in tune with their search for meaning. Jesus' single-mindedness in the face of impending suffering and death, reflected in the gospel's repeated stress that his "face was set toward Jerusalem," is perhaps the ultimate case in point of such focus.

• *Knowing and doing.* Christians who demonstrate wholeness don't get tangled up in arguments about "faith" and "works." They have embraced and synthesized the givens of both Paul and James. They "walk the talk"; they live the language of faith.

• *Risk-taking.* Through the personal strength with which God has equipped them, whole persons can risk intimacy with others, open themselves to criticism, to learning new things, to love, to tenderness. "I can do all things through Christ who strengthens me," said Paul; and he certainly tried many of them, taking great risks for the Lord in the process.

• *Self-acceptance.* The whole person's self-image and self-esteem are well enough intact to supply him or her with the energy necessary for a self-emptying life-style. Peter—whose impetuosity and mistakes are written large in the gospels and Acts—certainly had to come a long way in order to be able to say, "You are a chosen people, a royal priesthood, a holy nation, a people belonging to God." This image of himself and the church was fundamental to his development of the theme of his first letter, shot through as it is with the call to suffer for Christ's sake.

Given what we have been saying about the dynamics of how a person becomes addicted to a substance, a relationship, or a behavior pattern, the disparity between addiction and wholeness is obvious. How do we effectively help the addict—and in this chapter our major focus is on the alcoholic—move toward realizing the freedom which comes with being a whole person?

We have already spoken of the indispensable role to be played by the church. The obvious answer that will thus occur to many people is "by preaching and teaching." That's a correct answer—as far as it goes. But educators have long recognized that optimum learning takes place by doing. Action is the key word. In the case of a recovering alcoholic, the action is going to meetings, "working the steps," getting a sponsor, helping other alcoholics.

What is the relationship between the understanding of addiction we have been developing and the church's response to alcoholism? Prevention is one dimension of the answer; confrontation and early intervention make up the other. And, especially in more conservative churches, this raises the issue of the relationship between pastoral care and church discipline as these focus on the needs of the alcoholic and his or her family within the church.

This is no mere detail of ecclesiological theory. To see how complicated a question it is, ask yourself this: When does the agent of sin become sin's victim? To see how crucial it is, ask it this way: How can the church successfully intervene for the good of the body as well as for the good of the family of the alcoholic?

The ecclesiastical community has not often recognized how complex a disorder addiction to beverage alcohol is. Consequently, its traditional address to the problem among its members has been simplistic and woefully inadequate. In short, too little is offered too late. The point at which an addiction problem has been recognized and confronted has usually been when the parishioner is already on the ecclesiastical skids through his self-imposed ostracism. These persons are most often referred to treatment when the church and the family have all but thrown up their hands in disgust or defeat.

The church's traditional simplistic approach has been one in which we harbor thoughts and feelings about the alcohol-addicted person as morally inferior and thus lacking in the will-power to control his or her impulses. Because he or she failed to correct long out-of-control drinking behaviors, the church finally, in loveless exasperation, excommunicates. To this righteous official response of the church is appended, almost as an afterthought, a tardy and tawdry attempt at a show of grace in the hope for repentance. But the words of excommunication — if noticed at all by the addict — are received bitterly, and the addict usually spends the rest of his or her existence living out and acting out that resentment.

There is little to choose between this rigorously righteous approach and that of the church which turns not only its cheek, but its head and good sense as well. The litany of copouts is familiar: "Ignore it." "Pray for the brother." "Give it a little time." "It's not *that* bad." (I ask, "not *how* bad?") "Perhaps the marriage is the problem: work on the marriage." Admonitions are non-existent. No one would think of saying, point blank, "Your drinking is a problem." Patience degenerates into sloth, tolerance into faintheartedness. Love washes into sentimentality. Such a non-approach to pastoral care for alcoholics cries out for the child who proclaimed, "The emperor has no clothes!"

What is needed is an understanding of beverage alcohol addiction as well as a perspective on ecclesiastical discipline that has as its focus reconciliation to Christ and restoration to a functional place to stand within the Christian community.

Achieving that understanding of alcohol addiction is not helped along by definitions which suggest that it is "a primary progressively pathological constitutional reaction to ingestion of beverage alcohol; psychosocial symptoms are secondary, derivative and progressive, regardless of premorbid psychosocial antecedents"[9] — even if they are translated into everyday English. The church ought not to let go of its insistence that alcoholism has serious moral dimensions. Addiction is not simply a disease. An addict is not simply a choiceless victim.

More helpful is the understanding of alcohol addiction as a sinful behavioral disorder involving the abuse of ethanol, which inevitably produces or exaggerates serious psychosocial or physical problems. Note that the element of "choice" does not figure in this definition. Choice and loss of choice represent the extremes of a continuum on which all kinds of alcoholisms can be plotted. That this is a continuum makes it evident that alcoholism is a *progressive* disorder. The alcoholic doesn't stand on one spot but moves along the line until an intervention stops the progression of the disease.

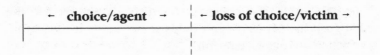

| ← **choice/agent** → | ← **loss of choice/victim** → |

But the church's insistence on the "moral issue," as it hammers out its perspective on pastoral care/discipline, does not necessarily close it to consistent evidence from the scientific community that alcoholism also has physical, chemical, and metabolic dimensions to it. Already in 1970, research indicated that "hyperactivity in the central nervous system following alcohol withdrawal demonstrates the development of physical dependence upon alcohol."[10] The evidence is incontrovertible. Alcohol addicts cross the line from being an agent of what they do to themselves—spiritually, physically, socially, and psychologically—to being a victim of the abuse they have perpetrated on themselves.

Whose task is it to determine when that line is crossed? The religious community or the scientific community? Both will have their say. The scientific community, we have noted, tends to be biased toward the view that the alcoholic is the victim of a disease. The church is probably as one-sided in seeing the alcoholic as an agent of sin, morally inferior and spiritually weak.

The agent/victim dilemma may strike us as an intellectual puzzle to be solved by choosing one or the other explanation. But it only reflects what we encounter often: what we know as the truth of something is elliptical; it has two focal points. We have free will; we are within the divine will. We are good; we are evil. We are saved by grace, not by works; but show me a person's works in life and I will see grace operative.

In point of fact, drawing a sharp line between "victim" and "agent" is difficult and usually unnecessary. Alcohol addicts are *always* victims and *always* agents. Although they may be victimized by their addiction, they are responsible for the progression of the disorder, for the consequences of their behavior, and ultimately for getting into treatment. On the other side, although they may be the agents of their own alcohol abuse and for the tragedies that lie in the wake of that abuse, they are also victimized by physiological givens (TIQ) that precipitate loss of choice, entrapment to ethanol, and bondage to it.

As victim or as agent, the alcoholic is still in need of Christ's ministry. Forgiving sins and healing the sick (note that he made a close link between these; Mark 2:3-12), Jesus was present "full of grace and truth" when he "dwelt among us," and he expects his body to be present in the world full of his grace and truth. Galatians 6:1 sums up Paul's insight into how the church can be this kind of community in a way that is especially pertinent to our discussion of addiction.

In Galatians 5, Paul has been discussing the freedom of the Christian—a powerful theme of that epistle. In summary, Paul teaches that justification through Christ has set us free from the law. We are under no obligation to do the law *in order* to gain our righteous standing before God. This freedom of the Christian is not for us to abuse but to use—and Paul's primary suggestion for its use is in loving one another (v. 13). Paul follows this with a discussion of the tension between "flesh" and "spirit," based on his insistence on our freedom. We are led by the Spirit into freedom, not compulsion. This happy circumstance is invaded by the still-present reality of the flesh (Paul isn't referring here only to sins of the physical body, as the list in v. 21 shows), which stands in contrast to and in competition with the Spirit. We are encouraged to walk by the Spirit, careful not to play a game of spiritual "one-upmanship" or "mine is better than yours" (v. 26).

In fact, chapter 6 then begins, "If any man is *caught up* in a trespass, you who are spiritual should restore him in a spirit of gentleness. Look to yourself, lest you too be tempted." The term

Paul uses here to describe the phenomenon of "entrapment" by sin is especially pertinent for our discussion.

The basic meaning of the verb is to "grasp" or to "seize." In the active voice, it denotes the action of "taking"; in the passive it suggests acceptance or reception from another. Its deeper meaning has the connotation of ownership or integration or assimilation into one's self. The usage in Galatians 6:1 suggests a fault into which a brother is betrayed unaware, so that it is not *intentionally* wrong.[11] His entrapment becomes a condition, not an isolated event.

Paul's description of being caught up in an unmanageable condition of powerlessness speaks to the dynamics of addiction. No child or young person ever plans to be an addict when he or she grows up. Yet a learned behavior becomes a habit that eventually overwhelms them—to the detriment of whatever plans they have made. Their addiction also snares people close to them. The parent or spouse or employer may find himself or herself caught up in several games in relationship to the addict: protecting, denying, vilifying, lying, self-pitying, dominating, or even depending on the addict's dependency. All are tentacles of the addiction syndrome which reach out and touch other people besides the addict. All are agents; all are victims.

The answer to addiction Paul gives in Galatians 6:1 is gentle restoration. That phrase demonstrates the cutting edge of a dynamic tension between pastoral care and ecclesiastical discipline with which the agent/victim dilemma of addiction needs to be confronted.

Ecclesiastical discipline cannot be separated from pastoral care. Church discipline is part of the gospel, an inescapable consequence of the discipling process we call the proclamation of the good news of the kingdom of God.[12] The goal of discipline is *restoration*. The medium is gentleness. The context is a community of caring members of Christ's body. The means of discipline range widely, from Jesus' advice to Peter that he should "forgive seventy times seven" (Matthew 18:22) to Paul's consignment of an offender to Satan (1 Corinthians 5:5).

One reason the church often fails in the exercise of *discipline* with the alcoholic is its failure to grasp the distinction between church discipline and punishment. It either seeks to punish instead of restore, to coerce instead of proclaim the good news;

or it simply "hopes for the best" without grounding that hope in the Word of God.

Brunner warns against the serious consequences when the function of church discipline falls into disuse: "This absence of any kind of church discipline inevitably gives the impression that to belong or not to belong to the Church comes to the same thing in the end, and makes no difference in practical life."[13]

Without confrontation and the expectation of confession and repentance, there can be no opportunity for forgiveness and restoration. And without forgiveness, the church has nothing to say. Forgiveness and deliverance from sins is the basis, the sum, the criterion, of all that may be called the Christian faith and life. Christian life is the life which takes a person out of himself or herself and introduces the principle of divine life.[14]

Discipline must be exercised in order for the church to maintain its distinction from the world; it must be exercised in order to call forth its own from the world. Our reluctance to exercise the "power of the keys" would be diminished if we could integrate into the life of the church a commitment to understand discipline as a proclamation of good news, not bad.

The church has the right—indeed, the *duty*—to get involved in the intervention process by which the addicted person gets treatment. If a person is caught up in a trespass, he or she must be dealt with gently for purposes of restoration. But this concern for "gentleness" is not a suggestion that if things get complicated we can avoid dealing with them. There is a parallel here with Paul's discussion of "love" in 1 Corinthians 13. "Love is kind," the apostle says. Kind, yes; but not wishy-washy. Foolish kindness or gentleness is in fact cruel. To cover up repeatedly for the addict, always cleaning up after his or her messes, doing one's best to ward off the consequences of irresponsible behavior, only gives the addict tacit permission to do it again.

Graham Greene's novel *The Heart of the Matter* tells the story of Scobie, who has an affair with a very plain woman. Lewis Smedes says of Scobie: "Too 'kind' to leave his wife or tell her about the affair, he is also too kind to leave the mistress. Such 'kindness' reflects not love but pity." Dishonest kindness or gentleness is poisonous. Authentic kindness and gentleness is always a move toward healing.[15]

Toughness is not always out of tune with kindness. Kindness is not always gentle. Gentleness can be hard. Gentle kindness means permitting an addict to suffer the pain of withdrawal in order to precipitate the crisis necessary for a change in life-style. Gentleness does not preclude tough talk or firm action. It is an attitude of the heart which says: "I love you and care for you so much that I will not allow you future hurt by providing a quick fix for present pain."

In conclusion, I offer the following guidelines for congregations confronting the problem of addiction within their fellowship (and, whether or not they admit it, that includes most congregations):

1. Understand the nature of the addiction experience.

2. Understand that church discipline is a specific focus of pastoral care, whose goal is essentially restoration and forgiveness.

3. The person who represents the church on a pastoral call must be "trustfully" related to the offending brother or sister. Discipline is done by a brother to a brother or a sister to a sister. That relationship is not simply a formal or legal one but a dynamic and interpersonal one. Many efforts at church discipline fail because a formal visit is officially made on a stranger-to-stranger basis. Little wonder that for an addict, already paranoid and full of self-pity, such a formal encounter becomes just one more piece of data to document his or her experience of rejection—and feeds the process of projection of blame upon others.

4. Once there is even apparent evidence of a struggle with chemical dependency in a member of its fellowship, the church must be prepared to make the first call *quickly*.

5. The person making the call must have the offensive facts readily in hand, prepared to recount those facts before the offending person.[16]

6. The goal of the visit is to encourage treatment.

7. If after several visits and confrontations, the offending person is not yet willing to seek help for his or her problem, the church must boldly declare that he or she either receive the needed help or be formally cut off from fellowship with God's people.[17]

8. This action must include the clear statement that the church stands ready to receive the person if he or she seeks

needed help and owns his or her share of responsibility in the disorder.

9. During this process, the prayers and support of the church are solicited by way of public and bulletin announcements.

The guidelines suggested above attempt to reflect the understanding that the addict is both agent and victim. Addicted persons need treatment. They also need to be reconciled responsibly to Christ's body. That is part of the treatment, just as the treatment is part of the reconciliation.

These guidelines, stated briefly as they are, may seem cut-and-dried, cold and unfeeling. Play them, however, against the background of the following case. Can the grace of God incarnated in the life of the church be expressed by means of the "tough love" method outlined here? Are there better alternatives?

CASE STUDY

Don't Go Home, Brad

On the plane back to Boise that night, Dr. Schaeffer turned over in his mind the advice he had just given the elders of First Church in Lincoln. He had suggested that Bradley Riggins be given a specific outline of his responsibilities to his family and church and that he be held accountable for his behavior relative to these requirements or face termination from the church. He wondered if he was too harsh in his judgment of Brad and had been too extreme in his recommendation.

Lawrence Schaeffer was an addictions counselor for New Life Treatment Center. He had met Brad two years ago when he had checked into New Life broken, lost, and threatened with divorce due to alcohol abuse and the consequent neglect and physical abuse of his family.

Brad had undergone six months of treatment during residency at New Life. Dr. Schaeffer had been in regular contact with Brad's family and church while the treatment was going on, advising them that addiction is treatable and Brad could be helped if he would follow the prescribed demands of the program.

Kathy Riggins had been skeptical all along. "I've had it with Brad," she said. "Chip is afraid of him; after all, a twelve-year-old boy just doesn't forget it when his father pushes him through a window."

Dr. Schaeffer could understand Kathy's fear but had suggested *AL ANON,* a self-help group for spouses of alcoholics. "Give Brad a chance to recover," he had told her. "After all, this is the first time he has been treated for addiction."

"How would you like to be in my shoes?", Kathy had asked. "What would *you* do if someone threatened your life? Would you sleep with that person?"

"No," he had told her. "I would want that person to get help. And I would get help. And I would not live in that situation again until we both received help."

Kathy was not so sure. After six months of separation, she had been reluctant to risk putting herself back in the situation that had led to the separation in the first place. The church was, however, encouraged. The family's elder reminded Kathy of the Christian principles about marriage, forgiveness, and hope. Reluctantly—and not a little fearfully—she agreed to try again.

When Brad completed his six-month residency at New Life, his discharge notice read: "Prognosis is guarded. The staff did not see specific attitudinal, emotional, or spiritual changes that were significant. It is questionable whether Brad understands his addiction; and, in fact, he expresses a naive optimism about his recovery." "I'll never drink again" was the phrase he used. Dr. Schaeffer had heard it too often from those who later relapsed. "I'm afraid that statement is simply a gross denial of his alcoholism problem," he had told a colleague.

The results of Brad's return to his family were mixed. Kathy was cold and doubtful. She soon stopped attending *AL ANON.* She was a person with a worried frown on her face. Brad was unable to return to his former job as a cement truck driver because his driver's license, which had been revoked, was not returned to him. Consequently, he took odd jobs and got some financial help from his parents. He returned to First Church— almost arrogantly, announcing with bravado that "I'm just as good as anyone here; I belong." He failed to continue a program of recovery, refusing to attend AA meetings.

Six months later Dr. Schaeffer's fears were realized: Brad returned to drinking. He returned to New Life; but now Kathy filed for divorce. The marriage was over as far as she was concerned.

The church was reluctant to bless the decision but agreed not to discipline Kathy for it.

The church was in contact with New Life and received advice to put pressure on Brad to pay child support. While Brad was at New Life, he borrowed $800 from a gullible client and bought a car with the money. Confronted about borrowing money, buying a car, and not sending money home, Brad had shrugged his shoulders: "What can I say? I need the car to get to work so I can pay my bills."

Dr. Schaeffer discharged Brad from the residency program at New Life for his noncompliance with the treatment plan. Brad maintained some contact with New Life staff as an outpatient, consistently leaving them with the impression that he was "stagnant in his personal growth, a loner who lived in social isolation, not amenable to treatment or a changed behavior pattern."

One month after the divorce was final, Brad received his divorce papers. He talked over the situation with Dr. Schaeffer, who advised him to begin his life over in Boise, where New Life could provide necessary support and counsel. Brad was noncommittal: "I'll see."

In fact Brad returned to Lincoln, expecting that his parents, brothers and sisters, or even Kathy and the children might help, receive, or support him. The church, however, intervened to help Kathy enforce the court's decision: no visitation rights without child support. Brad was angered by this decision. When he received his first paycheck as a day laborer, he gave none of it to either his ex-wife or to his mother, with whom he was living, telling each one that he had to pay the other first.

The church no longer knew how to advise the Riggins family. They asked Dr. Schaeffer to come to Lincoln and advise them. This was the advice he had given the elders that evening:

1. Arrange a meeting with Brad's father and mother, ex-wife and children, Kathy's friend and supporter, and elders in order to get the facts: What did Brad do while drinking? What did he say? Remember, you are trying to convince Brad that he is not responsible, that he needs help to be responsible and that there are certain consequences for his irresponsibility.

2. After the facts are together in order invite Brad to a meeting to confront him with them. The family and other significant

persons in Brad's life should take their turn reciting the facts about Brad to him.

3. Communicate in words to Brad: "We cannot continue to stand by and watch while you go on hurting yourself and us. You can no longer use your mother and ex-wife as excuses for your drinking behavior and lack of support. Listen to how we see you. . . . Because we love you, Brad, you must leave the fellowship of your children and church and return only when you show evidence of repentance: full payment of back child support, repayment of the financial loans from mother and father; a successful move into your own apartment; a steady job for one year; and participation in AA. If you do not follow these instructions, we have no option but to excommunicate you from the fellowship of believers.

The elder in charge of the meeting countered this advice with a question: "After hearing Brad's mother rise up and accuse the church of a lack of compassion, what shall we say, Dr. Schaeffer?"

The doctor paused. "It's a cruel love that knows no limits for the beloved. Brad won't get well if we rescue him and fail to hold him accountable."

"But isn't he sick, Doctor?", the elder asked. "It just doesn't seem Christlike to turn a sick man out into the cold like that."

Dr. Schaeffer wondered himself. Maybe with a little more patience and tolerance Brad might make it. "Was I advising a method that was unreasonably harsh?"

QUESTIONS FOR FURTHER REFLECTION:

1. Is Bradley Riggins, whom Dr. Schaeffer and the elders of First Church are attempting to help, any more in need of the tough love approach than is Jim Sloan (*see the Case Study at the end of Chapter 3*)?

2. The moral/behavioral perspective on alcohol addiction offers the alcoholic an opportunity to reflect on his disease in a way that goes beyond the "disease concept." How?

3. What answer would you give to the question the elder posed to Dr. Schaeffer? Has his tough love approach gone beyond the boundaries of compassion?

4. Is excommunication from the church ever a viable option or a key to be used in the treatment of an addicted person? What would you say to the argument that this final step of discipline is much too harsh, and that under the circumstances, Bradley Riggins probably could not care less about his relationship to the church, except to milk its resources?

CHAPTER V

RELIGION AND ADDICTION

At first glance one might suppose that "religion" would fit into a study of the addiction experience not as a facet of the problem but as the concluding chapter—the one which proposes solutions. Indeed, in many cases religious activity is a joyful and healthy celebration of life that is congruent and well integrated. But the enjoyment of beverage alcohol can be a healthful experience, too. If a healthy expression of religious experience points beyond the dead end of Freud's assumption that religion is simply a universal neurosis, it is nevertheless evident that some religious experience, because of its addictive manifestations, can also support Freud's conclusions.

Just as it was not our intention to distinguish smooth and suave sexual technique from cloddish and clumsy one-night stands, nor sipping vintage wine from gulping rotgut on Skid Row, the point of this chapter is not to sort out good religion from bad or orthodoxy from heterodoxy. Nor is this chapter written to vindicate Christianity as *the* answer to addiction, although the discussion here of religion and addiction is carried on in the framework of historic Christianity, and its presuppositions reflect the principles of the Christian tradition.

My purpose is not to offer an apology for Christ. He does not need my apology. He is who he is, the Beginning and the End. What we do with him between the times, however, is often a tragicomic roadshow of religious one-upmanship, distortion, and addiction.

The comparison between alcohol and God is scarcely a new discovery. Long ago, in *The Varieties of Religious Experience,* William James noted the similarity of function:

> The sway of alcohol over mankind is unquestionably due to its power to stimulate the mystical faculties of human nature, usually crushed to the earth by the cold facts and dry criticisms of the sober hour. Sobriety diminishes, discriminates, says, "no"; drunkenness expands, unites, and says "yes." It is in fact the great exciter of the "yes" function in man. The drunken consciousness is but one bit of the mystical consciousness.[1]

Much earlier still, St. Paul seems to have been aware of this relationship. He mandated the Ephesian Christians (5:18) not to be drunk with wine but to be filled with the Spirit.

Thomas Wolfe described one of the characters in his classic novel *Look Homeward, Angel* like this: "In all the world there was no other like him. No other like him to be so sublimely and majestically drunken. Why, when it was possible to buy God in a bottle and drink him off and become a God oneself, were men not forever drunken?"[2]

Howard Clinebell, who wrote extensively and insightfully about alcoholism in the 1950s, reflected on what is often the common denominator between alcohol and religion. Because of the intensity of our negative feelings toward drunkenness many of us tend to overlook the fact that alcohol is an answer to a problem area in life when religion also gives an answer.[3] Both religion and alcohol offer an answer to weariness, boredom and drudgery, rejection and loneliness, fear, meaninglessness, and a sense of anomie. Bellying up to the bar for another glass of fire-brewed magic and shuffling up to the altar for the mystical host are not altogether unrelated motions. Camaraderie happens in the fellowship hall after the morning service and in the cocktail lounge during "happy hour." Chemical intoxication and spiritual euphoria are akin. It was no accident that the newly anointed apostles on Pentecost morning were mistaken for common drunks on the street.

In a letter to Bill W., co-founder of Alcoholics Anonymous, the Swiss psychologist Carl Jung wrote: "Craving for alcohol is the equivalent on a low level of the spiritual thirst of our being for wholeness or union with God. . . . Alcohol in Latin is *spiritus* and you use the same word for the highest religious experience as well as the most depraving poison."[4]

In terms of purpose and of the emotion felt, getting high on Jesus and getting high on Jim Beam are similar experiences. There is the exhilaration, the freedom, the flow of feeling, the escape from reason and from the painful obsession with what wearies us with worry. We ask Jesus to do what we ask booze to do: make us feel better fast. Ken Medema's song "Corner Drugstore Jesus" puts into words what many people expect Christianity to do for them:

> *Do you want a corner drugstore Jesus,*
> *Passing happiness pills?*
> *Do you want some kind of magic pot*
> *That will cure all your ills?*

The biblical figure of Simon the magician (Acts 8) reminds us that this kind of religion was not invented by the "me generation." But its prevalence today lends substance to the claim that religion has addicting qualities, or, to put it more precisely, that our addiction-prone selves are drawn to using religion in an addictive manner, because it makes us feel better. There is warrant for describing the dangers of addictive religion in terms similar to what Clinebell says of alcoholism: it can "interfere frequently or continuously with important life adjustments, interpersonal relationships, and general well-being."[5] Religion can get us high in the same way as romance can put us in the clouds. And like romance, religion can become an object of obsession that causes serious life problems. Or it can be used appropriately, giving us—particularly during worship—an experience that strengthens our resolution to be wholly directed by the Holy Other.

Persons who take their religious practice seriously are vulnerable to becoming addicted to their religion in a harmful way. Religious consumption can become sick. Many people have suggested that liquor bottles ought to carry a government warning that alcohol may be addictive and injurious to your health. Perhaps religious fellowships ought to include a sign on their buildings and a notice in their literature notifying prospective disciples that adherence to this religion may be harmful to their health.

The language of addiction, we have seen again and again, is the language of dependency. So someone might retort to our suggestion that religion is potentially addictive by asking: "But doesn't God *want* us to depend on him?" Some people might suggest that the answer to that is easy. "Of course," they will say, citing any of a number of Scripture texts to the effect of "Cast all your cares on him." But I would contend that God wants us to be free from a dependent relationship with him.

The point at issue here is not the nature of God but what we understand by *dependency on God.* No doubt that God wants us for our own good to acknowledge our creatureliness, to experience the limits to our freedom, and come to terms with our inevitable finitude. Every newborn baby is an eloquent testimony to human createdness. As we discussed in Chapter 2, our freedom is hedged about with questions and most assuredly limited, particularly by the brute and brutal fact that it is impossible for us to get out of life alive.

Does God then want us to fly to his bosom, cling to the cross, finger our beads, or simply fold our hands and pray? Recall that Jesus sent out his disciples to do the work of the kingdom, and when a contingent reported failure he chastised them for lack of faith. There lies the other side of the paradox of dependency on God. Limited, finite creatures as we are, we are told to go forth in Christ and conquer in his name—to be accountable, to be responsible, to heal the sick, to cast out demons, to forgive sins. Surely we must acknowledge our Creator, Redeemer, Sustainer. Surely we must remember who it is that butters our bread and stirs our drink. But he has equipped us to tend his garden, feed his lambs, and replenish his earth, through the power of his Spirit, a power which has taken up residence in every true believer.

So the choice is not between "dependence" and "independence" as such, but between harmful dependence on religious beliefs and practices and a dynamic religious experience keynoted by God's equipping act, which sets us free to incarnate in our setting the Love that was incarnated in Jesus Christ on behalf of the whole world.

It is not, as J. B. Phillips observes, that critics of Christianity are completely incorrect when they call religious faith a form of psychological escape.[6] A dose of escapism can be the balm that religion legitimately provides a suffering soul. God is the refuge and strength for many saints who have made the Word of God their meat and drink. God is a safe harbor for all who have forsaken every worldly attachment, considering it garbage by comparison with the "higher calling." Not everyone who has used religious faith as an escape is a religious addict. Nor is every business executive who pours down a gin and tonic after a hard day at the office an alcoholic.

What criterion, then, differentiates the neurotic, dependency-prone religious addict from the faithful, mature believer? If we think of human personalities as being placed along a continuum from the rootless self at one end to the well-defined or centered self on the other, the mature believer is found toward the right-hand side, in the direction of the centered self. For such a believer, what might be called escaping to God is in fact more akin to drawing living water from a well, a source of strength that enables one to venture back onto the streets of his existence.

Jesus gave no indication during his earthly ministry that his bosom was fair game for the terminally anxious looking for a way to ride out the storm. The easy yoke he invited the religiously oppressed to carry was the yoke of discipleship. Those staggering under the burden of religious obligations were not summoned to the perpetual weightlessness of a ride on a spiritual space shuttle but to a life of serving the Lord with gladness.

Why are taverns dark? We have been socialized to believe that it is for "atmosphere"—that primitive conviviality is enhanced when the lights are turned down low. But there is also a psychological reason. Many a tavern dweller feels a sense of security in the shadows, because they decrease the chances of being seen by the hostile forces and powers that would otherwise capture one, blame one, somehow "get" one. The darkened tavern is a safe place to be. It may be a long way from Jesus' bosom, but it fulfils the same function of escape from the painful present.

There is more to escapist religiosity than simply its use as a release from situations of stress. In an earlier chapter we spoke of Erich Fromm's contention that religion represents an escape from freedom. On the agenda of every addict is a purposeful avoidance of responsibility. That may be covered up by layers of bluff and tough talk, and in many cases by behavior that seems willfully to flout conventional expectations. But the addict secretly abhors the responsibility inherent in power and freedom. The escape from freedom is on the hidden agenda even as an obsession with freedom and power is on the open agenda. He may openly talk about the need for decisive action in getting U.S. troops into or out of Central America, but finds it difficult to drag himself out of bed in the morning to face another day at the office.

Fromm's point is that religion contends with this paradox. The Protestant Reformation exposes it. Its thrust for freedom and autonomy over against the medieval church produced another kind of bondage within the framework of the doctrine of total depravity. When the Reformation released people from the crushing authority of the medieval church, it turned them face to face with their own inadequacy and powerlessness before the judgment seat of a righteous God. The medieval church stressed human dignity through the freedom of the will and the efficaciousness of human striving toward righteousness. The Reformers took the keys of authority out of the hands of the church and put them into the hands of the individual believer. But this apparent victory for individual autonomy and dignity was erased by the doctrine of total depravity and human powerlessness over our sinful condition. According to Fromm, the doctrines of ecclesiastical authority in the Middle Ages and of depravity in the Reformation performed the same function of offering escape from freedom.[7] Hence they enhanced the possibilities of addiction to a religious "fix."

There is an important insight here, though I think Fromm failed to acknowledge how the Reformers did grapple with the tension between human powerlessness in the face of evil and responsibility to obey the moral law in the context of grace. A robust and healthy religious attitude will let that paradox stand without trying to fix it. Pathological religious addiction, on the other hand, will either obsessively insist on absolute freedom or fly to Jesus' bosom, content to let the world go by . . . or go to hell.

The art of psychotherapy has contributed to the maintenance of this paradox between freedom and dependency, responsibility and powerlessness. David Roberts reminds us of its contribution toward increasing man's capacity to solve his own problems, both by deepening the diagnosis and by tapping hitherto latent resources. And from this standpoint, theology richly deserves criticism whenever it equates human "goodness" with slavish dependence upon the arbitrary will of a celestial tyrant who treats His creatures in a way that any humane person would regard as abominable.[8]

Theology is equally culpable when it fosters the belief that human persons are wholly incapable of any good. Colorful if well-worn imagery which speaks or sings of the sinful human as a moral worm and food for worms may, if diligently explained, convey an important truth about the human condition—but at a considerable risk to those who are not experienced or equipped or psychologically disposed to hear in such language anything more than divinely sanctioned confirmation of their own sense of worthlessness. Such souls tend to give up on themselves and become vulnerable to any religious fantasy that offers to pull them out of the pit of powerlessness. This is a particular attraction of those cults which enable people to live vicariously through a powerful leader. Not the least of the reasons for the success of cults is their aptitude for picking clean the moral bones (and money belts) of religious addicts who have been force-fed dogmas which explore and deplore human depravity but do not at the same time celebrate the inestimable value God places on us in Christ. It is true that such notions may have been more caught by particularly vulnerable spirits than taught to them . . . but somebody threw the ball.

Harry Tiebout, a psychiatrist who devoted his career to helping alcoholics, wrote that while "psychotherapy can unlock some of the healthy resources and potential within the tormented soul, religion can also release the positive potential which resides in the unconscious, freeing the person to meet life anew."[9] This claim—made, remarkably, forty years ago, at a time when psychoanalysis reigned supreme as queen of the unconscious—reinforces the point that religious experience in itself is not necessarily sick or addictive. It can at its best deepen the human experience of personal freedom within the framework of faith in God. But the healthy religious experience presupposes that a balance is maintained between two extremes:

mindless and neurotic dependence on God and arrogant rejection of the God who is there.

Freud articulated the former of these extremes in terms of "religion as projection." The child grows up to the discovery of being destined to remain a child forever. Anxiety over this leads to the further discovery that one cannot do without some protection against unknown and mighty powers. Thus is born the projection of the father figure in cosmic proportions. The god created is one who can be both feared and appeased.[10] Characteristic of religious illusion is that it is derived from human wish. Freud is not making a theological evaluation that will distinguish true religion from false. He simply contends that *all* religion is generated by the wish for protection. Thus the believer guards against neurotic guilt and a fear of the principalities and powers.

While Freud's writings point to the neurotic element in addictive religion, the testimony of his life reflects the other extreme we mentioned: a tenuous and uncomfortable rejection of God. Freud was scared to death of death.[11] His own addiction to religion shines through his assessment of sick religion and his obsession with writing about religion and death. Theologian Hans Küng writes that Freud "fought deliberately against certain spiritual trends within himself. He seems to have been in a state of searching and painful conflict in which the positivist scholar (conscious) and the potential believer (unconscious) fought an open battle."[12]

The claim of the anxious agnostic or the antagonistic atheist that God is dead is often a religious claim, accepted on faith rather than rational proof. And this kind of religion can be as addictive as faith in God. The fantasy world or unconscious world of this addict surfaces in the expression of irrational fears. Better that God were dead; then we wouldn't have to deal with him. Freud protested too much—as do many addicts who religiously reject religion. Even as the compulsive believer is energized by a fear of freedom, so a compulsive atheist is energized by a fear of dependency. Freud discussed his problem with death in terms of ambition, striving to overcome death rather than to yield to its process by trusting or submitting to a Power greater than himself.

Addiction to religion and addiction to belief in a world come of age without God are not as esoteric as they might appear at first glance. The fact is that the average street peddler-heroin addict and the religious addict have remarkably similar personality characteristics and worldviews.

In their significant study of how a painful consciousness of life characterizes the outlooks and personalities of adolescent heroin addicts,[13] Isidor Chein and his colleagues found a clear constellation of traits: (1) a fearful and negative worldview; (2) low self-esteem; (3) a sense of inadequacy in dealing with life; (4) an inability to find involvement in work, personal relationships, and institutional affiliations rewarding. These adolescents were habitually anxious about their own worth. They systematically avoided novelty and challenges and responsibility, and welcomed relationships in which they were dependent. In essence, they were ripe for a burning.

The youth in Chein's study found what they were looking for in a hit on heroin. It might as easily have come in a fixation on religion. Significantly, the charismatic renewal has become highly attractive to young people even as students of adolescent behavior chart an almost epidemic abuse of alcohol and other drugs. In an age of anxiety the young are turning to religious fixes as well as chemical fixes to handle their fears. When addicts give themselves over, whether to heroin or to the religious cult leader, they are able to suppress their anxiety and sense of inadequacy.

Some readers might concede that religion can be addictive but argue that a person who chooses religion to handle anxiety has certainly made a less harmful decision than the one who opts for heroin or alcohol. On the face of it, one might think so; and the physical risks of addiction to religion are not likely to be comparable with the hazards of using heroin or alcohol. But addiction to religion is by no means harmless.

Of course, not every declaration of religious faith or commitment to religious truth or expression of religious fervor will inevitably degenerate into harmful dependence. We have made no such declaration regarding the use of alcoholic beverages either. But there are risk factors in the use of religions just as there are risks in the use of alcohol and other drugs.

We have been discussing harmful dependence, the process of addiction, as something which eventually robs the person of freedom of choice and ultimately causes serious life problems.

Addiction to religion may deprive a person of freedom by substituting a mindless dependence on the religious leader, or on religious ritual, or even on religious doctrine. A parallel attraction of ritual among heroin addicts emerged in research by Stanton Peele, who discovered that many of them would rather not see heroin legalized if it meant eliminating the injection procedures. The ritual associated with heroin becomes a crucial part of the drug experience.[14]

Another risk in religion comes from the willingness to accept magical solutions that are altogether irrational. "God will answer my prayer to be delivered from the unhappy situation in which I find myself if I am obedient to his will" is a distortion of prayer and a misappropriation of the religious truth that God upholds us by his providence.

The error here is not the belief that God cares for those whom he has created, but the notion that this care will take the form of a magical intervention from outside if we will just deploy the right gimmicks: obey the rules and pray. A healthy religious perspective on obedience to God is that of the Psalmist: "Oh, how I love thy law! It is my meditation all the day" (Psalm 119:97). For the Psalmist, obedience was grounded in an experience of grace and realized in the framework of mercy, not magic.

The tendency to play down—to the point of exclusion—all individual effort is another risk involved in religious practice which is moving toward addiction. The temptation is to eliminate the paradox in religious truth. But "I surrender all," despite its noble sound, is sentimental trash, symptomatic of a pathological religious experience, unless it is followed up and counterbalanced by the readiness for engagement in life: "Am I a soldier of the cross?"

With these more general comparisons of addiction to religion with addiction to drugs, let us now look more closely at religious preoccupation with dogma, ritual, and God. As we do so, it is important to remember that any activity becomes addictive when the experience erases a person's awareness, when it provides predictable and immediate gratification, when it is used not to gain pleasure but to avoid pain, when it damages self-esteem, when it destroys other involvements and obliterates any or all life-integrating principles and perspectives.

Perhaps the most powerful critique of religion in this century was that of the man whom many would call the greatest contemporary theologian, Karl Barth. According to Barth, the inadequacy of religion must be viewed in the light of God's revelation of himself. In an extended discussion of the "Revelation of God as the Abolition of Religion," Barth defines religion as the human attempt to find God.[15] If this quest were able to succeed, he says, God's revelation of himself in Jesus Christ would have been unnecessary. Thus religion expresses the godless human effort to make up for our lack of God on our own terms.

The point of contact between Barth's discussion and the way we have been characterizing addiction is the self-will that insinuates itself on the life of faith. Recovering alcoholics often refer to themselves as victims of the "self-will run riot" syndrome.[16] The addict is fixated on the need to do whatever it takes to be fully human on his or her own terms, in his or her own way, and under his or her own power. Religion, as Barth defines it, is a similar attempt to justify oneself. It becomes a self-centered way to erect barriers against God, precluding an authentic relationship with him and producing at the same time frenzied efforts to overcome the gap between oneself and God. More religious fervor. *Compulsive* religious fervor.

Such religiosity reveals its own inadequacies to itself and produces reactions against itself. One of these reactions is mysticism; another is atheism. These are the extreme responses to the failure to get at God via a religious route. An extreme reaction to a failure is classic addictive behavior.

Paul Tillich was another twentieth-century theologian whose writings level sharp criticism against the religious fix. His well-known phrase "the Ground of Being" points to Tillich's contrast of authentic religion with idolatrous or addictive religion.

Tillich's concern is less with the religious quest itself than with the object of that quest. All religious quests, says Tillich, are concerned with the power of the New Being. When we invest ultimate concern in that which is Ultimate, we experience anxiety and awe in the face of the New Being. This is normal anxiety. It grows out of our realization that we are finite, mortal beings who encounter meaninglessness in the proximate things of life. Authentic religion reflects a congruency between the quest for ultimate reality and the New Being which is Ultimate Reality.

By contrast, when we invest our ultimate concern in that which is not ultimate but temporal and transitory, we absolutize the finite.[17] We are running after fixes that fix nothing. Absolutized and closed, religious truths become dead dogmas. We hover over them as a mourner lingers neurotically over the grave of a lost loved one, or as an intoxicated alcoholic stares blankly into what was once a bottle of exquisite bourbon. Both the religious dogmatist and the inebriated alcoholic keep looking for the life once promised, but now experience only the ashes of disillusionment and emptiness. The risk of giving ourselves over to these proximate concerns that religion always fusses about until they become idols is no merely imaginary threat.

Take the raging recent debate among evangelical Christians over the authority and interpretation of the Bible. This "battle for the Bible" is often presented as a central theological issue, occasionally as a philosophical one, and less often as a matter of presuppositions. I would suggest that there is also an addictive element tucked between the pages of all this heady discussion. And at the core of that addictive element is *fear:* the fear that the truth of God will be hidden, equivocated, or bastardized. In the heat of debate presuppositional statements or philosophical propositions or doctrinal utterances are idolized and mistakenly assigned positions of ultimate concern. Pathological fixations on "biblical inerrancy" suck the life out of a lively theological debate. Complicated issues on which devout and thoughtful Christians disagree become polarized. They become either-or litmus tests of orthodoxy. Extremists come out of the woodwork. Catcalls of heresy echo in the halls of synodical enclaves. It becomes a barroom brawl disguised as theological inquiry.

Idolatry and addiction have a lot in common. Tillich describes idolatry as elevating a preliminary concern to ultimacy. Something essentially conditional is taken as unconditional; something essentially particular is boosted to universality; something essentially finite is given infinite significance.[18] We don't carve idols from wood or stone or ivory anymore, of course. Often our mechanism is the projection of our wishes and fears on an external person who hears us, speaks to us, and acts for us. We are like Saul, who bet his life on what a medium could do for him (1 Samuel 28), asking her to produce Samuel. Understood thus, idolatry has less to do with religion than with getting what we want as quickly as possible—whether by throwing one's children into the fire, dancing around a golden calf, or sitting quietly in a pew, hymnbook in hand.

Hand in hand with the wishfulness in addictive patterns of religion comes fear. The wish that someone else will rescue me from perishing is couched in the fear that anyone who has the power to rescue me will also have the power to kill me. Religious fear can be terrifying, as anyone can attest who has watched a dying person agonize over physical pain that is intensified by paralyzing fears of eternity in hell—the product of rotten religious propaganda: "Scare the hell out of people and put the fear of God into them."

We might distinguish between the *surrendered* self of the person who has a healthy religious faith and the *capitulation* of the religious addict. The surrendered self does not go to God without a doubt, without a certain amount of kicking and screaming, without painful acknowledgment of a life-limiting dilemma. The capitulated self, on the other hand, religious hat in hand, grabs on to any power that happens by, caving in at the first promise of panacea that comes along. No doubts, no pain, no fuss, no muss.

Mass conversion experiences share certain elements with the "Woodstock Syndrome" of the late 1960s, in which hundreds of young people, transfixed and transformed by the pleasures of a rock concert in a grassy meadow, capitulated to the wonders of marijuna. "Come to the Saviour now; he gently calleth thee" holds forth an authentic Christian promise; but there are no "super-saver" discount fares. In the absence of gut-wrenching repentance and surrender, the painful experience of spiritual bankruptcy, "coming to the Savior" cannot establish a new pattern of growth for the whole person, but only the risk of religious addiction.

Any healthy religious response will include a certain measure of reflective resistance and even doubt. Frederick Buechner calls doubt the "ants in the pants of faith. They keep it awake and moving."[19]

Gordon Allport has distinguished sick religion from healthy religion in terms of interest, outlook, and the system of beliefs. He understands a religious sentiment as a disposition, built up through experience, to respond in certain habitual ways to conceptual objects and principles which one regards as of ultimate importance in one's own life. These habitual patterns of worship and belief do not necessarily make religion addictive. Harmful, addictive religion exhibits several specific characteristics, which we can identify, following Allport, as these:[20]

• Addictive religion is uncritical, unteachable, often arrogant. It is a closed system, swallowed whole without interpretation or reflection. A healthy religion, on the other hand, develops the believer's capacity to be flexible and self-critical. A defensive posture is built into the rabid religiosity of the addict. The typical alcoholic reflects a similar attitude: the world is all wrong, while I am all right.

• Sick religious experience specializes in magical thinking, self-justification, and personal comfort. Magic says: "Remember me, O Lord, your faithful servant, even as I have kept these commandments from my youth, thus providing me with the assurance that you will always be my God, defend my rights, and be on my side." Healthy religion, gratefully connected to God's grace, is other-directed, altruistic, straightforward. It is from this experience of God's unmerited favor that obedience flows.

• A sick religion becomes a means for rationalizing morally questionable behavior; the moral standards of a healthy religion are a cut above contemporary cultural morality. The addict specializes in rationalizing addictive behavior. "I went out and got drunk because the Tigers won the World Series." Or because they lost. To the extent that the addict's self-saving excuses can even be described as a "morality," it is an easy morality of convenience. A similar narcissism is at the root of sick religion. The way of sacrifice and self-denial is branded as out of touch, pietistic, fundamentalistic. What the religious addict is after is a balm from somewhere in Gilead, without having to bother about any commission from the master. This is the religious equivalent of fast food, the yearning to gulp down instant gratification. Preoccupied with self, the religious addict has no ear for inconvenient suggestions that "religion that is pure and undefiled before God is this: to visit orphans and widows in their affliction, and to keep oneself unstained from the world" (James 1:27).

• Religion which fosters a compartmentalization of life is sick; healthy religious practice offers a comprehensive philosophy of life. Religious addicts draw clear lines to banish ambiguity and shades of gray from their religious experience. Morality becomes a matter of a fixed code that makes no allowance for situations. Dogmas are fixed too. Formulas of subscription are drafted and signed to insure unreflective adherence to what is written in the doctrinal standards. Theological inquiry and honest discussion of issues are squelched in the name of orthodoxy. Rituals, ceremonies, and liturgical readings are standardized and rattled off.

The product of such religious experience is a compartmentalization of life. If religious experience can be limited to a regular time (Sunday morning) and place (the church sanctuary), the rest of life's affairs can be given free rein. Naturally, this is not the original intent of the regularities that compartmentalize religious expression. Quite the opposite, in fact, is intended: the provision of necessary controls on religious adherents. But the rigid compartmentalization of life inevitably spills the faithful out into the streets of the real world ill-equipped by an integrating principle of life. Without a worldview, people are free to raise hell where and when they please, so long as they pay their religious dues on Sunday.

This is addictive thinking. It is like the self-deception of those alcoholics who view themselves as "social drinkers" because they never take a drink on the job. Their efficiency rating may plummet—hungover in the mornings and inebriated in the afternoons following three-martini lunches—but they *never drink on the job*.

The nineteenth-century Danish religious thinker Søren Kierkegaard offered a profound diagnosis of sick religion. The most malignant form of religious addiction, he suggests, comes from perfectionistic expectations of our own selves.[21] The atheist philosopher Nietzsche put it this way: "There is no God. If there were, how could I stand it if I were not He?"[22] Caught between the necessity of humanity and the possibility of divinity, many people try to settle the tension instead of accepting it. They go for the gusto of the divine—and in the process are burned by the Wholly Other. Or, as Kierkegaard would put it, they get "drunk on infinitude."

Earl Jabaay discusses this phenomenon in terms of perfectionism. The human person reacts to finitude by getting caught up in the illusion of his or her own power.[23] It is sometimes ob-

served that an alcoholic is "the best worker on the line"—out of
the fear of being the worst of the lot. Compensation is the name
of that game, an overreaction to addictive practice. It is the age-
old problem of failing to accept the self as human, as a mere
mortal. This paradox of alcoholism has its parallel in the penchant of religious addicts for perfection. Acutely aware of their
own guilt and limitations, they overcompensate in their adherence to the tenets of their faith and practice. The joy is gone; the
celebration is forced. There is only the bug-eyed soul fixated on
its own attempt to be righteous . . . in its own eyes. Even the
announcement of grace becomes a trump card for works righteousness: I am not good enough to deserve so much grace. I do
not feel rotten enough to deserve so much grace. Is there anything I can do to measure up to such grace?

"Magical thinking," which we touched on earlier in talking
about the risks of religion, can be seen clearly in this attempt to
justify oneself before God. Understood theologically, magic (and
we are not referring here to such phenomena as "black magic"
or witchcraft or astrology) is based on the premise that the
outcome of every situation is the product of God and man
working in tandem. Life can be seen as a cosmic guessing game,
whose object is to determine God's purposes in history—either
world history or one's personal history. Magical thinking assumes
that the outcome of an event can be guaranteed by observing a
ritual or performing a ceremony ordered up by the village witch,
shaman, cult leader, or parish pastor.

Religious belief becomes a moralistic system of rewards and
punishments. It is a structured manipulation of God which rules
out faith in the face of the risks of the unknown and the uncontrollable. Some have figured out how to market such magic and
turn a good profit. Their consumers are victims of religious
addiction. Obsessive-compulsive life-styles become the hallmark
of their existence.

The addiction in such cases might be compared to that of
those alcoholics who judge their addiction to alcohol by the
clock. At one stage of this progressive illness, the chronic alcoholic will not touch a drink until the clock strikes 12:00 noon.
After all, only alcoholics drink in the morning; I can't be an
alcoholic, because I don't touch the stuff until after noon. Theological fallacy in that line of reasoning is evident; but "magical

thinking" disregards that and allows the alcoholic to suppose that the addiction can be controlled by observing the ritual of the clock. Another example of magical thinking in the world of the alcoholic is the claim that "I only drink beer, not the hard stuff," as if the ethanol in beer were not as potent as that in whisky or vodka.

The sources for magical thinking are sometimes explained sociologically with reference to the cultic role of the charismatic leader in a traditional village or the poverty and powerlessness which characterizes many of those attracted to cult figures today. On a deeper level, however, the village shaman and his contemporary equivalents are empowered by a phenomenon which is at the core of human existence: guilt. Guilt is an awesome breeder of magical thinking. It is the key that helps to open up the addictive dimension in religious experience.

E. Mansell Pattison, a psychiatrist who specializes in alcohol-related problems, classifies guilt into four categories that provide the makings not only of forgiveness and unforgiveness but also of a harmful addiction to religion:

1. *Civil Guilt.* Specific laws are broken and thus evoke an awareness of wrong-doing—often provoked by suffering the consequences (e.g., paying the fine for a traffic violation).

2. *Guilt Feelings.* These are subjective responses which produce feelings of self-criticism or, in extreme cases, self-condemnation.

3. *Existential Guilt.* This is the guilt of estrangement.

4. *Original Guilt.* This is the guilt of *being,* the internal experience of the fatal flaw.[24]

How we respond to this universal awareness of guilt is crucial for our emotional well-being. Religion can be a healing Word of grace that communicates the forgiveness of sins and the abolition of guilt. It can also be a club that wallops one into passive obedience, external compliance, internal resentment, and a profound sense of hopeless despair that is relieved obsessively—and therefore insufficiently—by one ritualistic fix or another. The keys of the kingdom, handed down through the years to the church, have been used masterfully to open people up to the mercy of God. They have also been used wickedly, to jam the door to the truth of grace. Religion gets sick, says Oates, when people are unwilling or unable to appropriate the forgiveness of

God and their fellow humans, or are unable or unwilling to forgive those from whom they are estranged.[25] So they erect a wall of resentment, isolating themselves from the reality of grace.

Reaction formations abound. Just as alcoholics undergo a profound personality change manifested while under the influence of ethanol, so the religious addict who has failed to integrate the vitality of grace into life may experience internally the exact opposite of what he or she expresses publicly. Religious zealotry, repeated confessions of sin, preoccupation with abstract doctrine, compulsive church involvement and attendance, frequent verbalization of religious jargon—all of these may mask the coldness of resentment, resistance to grace through faith, and the use of magic to manipulate God's favor.

Earlier we referred to the "battle for the Bible" among conservative evangelicals as a biblical-theological issue with a strong overlay of fear. It may also be seen as an example of guilt-induced magical thinking: will God be appeased, will his wrath be assuaged if I passionately defend the inerrancy and infallibility of his Scripture? Paul Tournier says,

> Belief in magic insinuates itself into our hearts. It rears its head as soon as we claim that a spiritual experience is the necessary condition that leads to true faith. We see that the frontier between authentic faith and magic is the frontier between humility and pride, between the humble search for God, and the proud claim to possess Him. This is the psychological cause of all the quarrels that divide Christians. It seems that the human mind is too small to grasp God in his fullness; so it clings to one of his attributes, one of his gifts, exaggerating its importance, and basing a system of belief on it. The Bible has its true value, but we end up by claiming to confine God in it.[26]

The elder brother in Jesus' story of the Prodigal Son (Luke 15) typifies religious zealotry. He covers a profound sense of guilt through suppressed rage, but eventually his resentment at having to work for the father comes out. Working for the father is a matter of working off a debt of guilt, and working hard enough will magically obliterate any obligation to him. The father's prodigious display of amazing grace to his younger brother unzips the magical mask the elder brother was wearing. He cannot tolerate the grace given to his wastrel sibling. All those years of hard labor for nothing! The whole time he had been convinced that his work alone would vindicate him; now he sees—to his dismay—that he was already vindicated by his father's love.

Is abolition of religion the answer to religious addiction? No more than that abolition of ethanol would eliminate alcoholism. Religion and ethanol are here to stay in any case. Besides, they are not the problem; people are. As far as religion is concerned, C. G. Jung points up the permanence of religious belief: "Man has always stood in need of the spiritual help which his particular religion held out to him. Man is never helped in his suffering by what he thinks of for himself; only suprahuman, revealed truth lifts him out of his distress."[27]

We started this chapter by asking whether God wants us to depend on him. We conclude that this question is not at issue. Our very existence presupposes dependence on him. We cannot run from our refuge and our strength, from him in whom we have our being. The real issue then is this: How do we manifest our dependence on God without being neurotically or addictively dependent on him? What is the shape of an appropriate response, reliance, and surrender to a higher power? Religion is sick if it is purely escapist; or if it is a flight from responsibility; or if it is a magical means to manhandle and manipulate God for our own narcissistic ends or to manipulate other people into passive submission (as cult leaders do); or if it is engendered by fear or guilt; or if it is an escape from freedom.

What is a healthy religious profile? How does one recover from a sick religion? These questions may be precluded by a prior one: What is the real danger involved in religious addiction? Few people ever die of it or go to jail for it. Religious addicts don't have to be corraled or picked up off the streets of our cities. Why all the fuss? It is certainly true that religious addiction does not lead to fatal head-on collisions on the highway—though it may cause a person to pull the trigger on someone after hearing "the voice of God" ringing in his ear. The religious addict may not lose a day's work from indulging in his or her passion the night before—but his or her productivity may be diminished by poor interpersonal relationships with peers. Religious addicts don't come home drunk at 3:00 A.M., but their obsessive involvement in "church work" can cause immeasurable suffering for their families. But if religious addiction's most serious debilitating effects cannot be compared with what alcohol abuse does, they are nevertheless tragic if one considers the loss of authentic personal faith as tragic; or if there is a spiritual blackout that blinds the person to the gracious long-suffering Father in heaven.

There is a cry for peace in every human being. The veil of rigid religiosity may shield us from the enlivening of the Son, the quickening of the Spirit, and the restfulness of the Father.

In Chapter 7, we consider how one can be free from this addiction to religion. What are the strategies for recovery? What shape does a healthy religious life-style take?

The following case study—again designed as a discussion-starter—helps to prepare for considering some of those questions.

CASE STUDY

Churchitis at Maple Avenue Church

"Have you considered a consultation at Pine Crest Mental Health Center?", Pastor Cowley asked his anxious parishioner.

Irene Matthews was shocked. "Me!" she cried. "A psychiatric hospital? Just when we were getting somewhere, you accuse me of being insane. If that's the way you feel, I am afraid that we have nothing more to say to each other. I am *so* hurt. Good day!"

The young pastor was bewildered as he left the Matthews home. What he had thought to be an incisive intervention had prematurely ended the session. More harm than good had come from this meeting. He began to doubt his pastoral intuition.

Irene Matthews was a charter member of Maple Avenue Church. She was a selfless laborer for the Lord, a faithful contributor in the Ladies Circle, a willing helper and teacher in Bible School, and a fine soprano voice in the choir. In her mid-forties, a little overweight, but cheerfully so, she went about her volunteer work at Maple Avenue with an enthusiasm that made her one of the most beloved people in the congregation. Pastor Cowley appreciated Irene—uneasily.

What had begun to bother him soon after his arrival at Maple Avenue were doubts about where Irene's faith was grounded.

She was always at the church, it seemed. If there was a job to do, Irene was there. No challenge was too difficult for her. Rarely did she ask for help on a project that obviously called for two or three people. Pastor Cowley remembered that Irene had taken on herself the responsibility for making half of the church's contribution to the annual community children's bazaar. She did it all without complaint that others did not pull their share of the work load.

Still, Pastor Cowley was concerned about Irene's motivation. What was the groundswell of strength for all her contributions? So he had decided to develop a deeper relationship with her. After several months of exchanging niceties about this and that, Irene had told him, "You know, Pastor, I am not the person everyone sees at church."

"Tell me about it, Irene."

She described a long history of depression and guilt over the death of her first child, Todd, from complications related to pneumonia. That had happened ten years ago, but Irene still held herself responsible for it.

George Matthews offered Irene little support. He seemed to handle the tragedy with only mild interest. A quiet, almost withdrawn man, he said nothing during Pastor Cowley's visits to the Matthews' home other than the ordinary greeting and farewell. The pastor wondered whether this silent treatment was a cover for some unresolved rage. Although George had never outwardly blamed Irene for Todd's death, she told the pastor that their relationship together had deteriorated to a barely tolerable existence with one another. He simply shook his head and walked out of the room when Irene would begin to talk about Todd. His only outlet, according to Irene, was an occasional drinking binge, but that—like Todd's death—was another taboo subject. Irene didn't dare confront George about his drinking, so she rationalized it: "He's entitled to a night out once in a while. You know, he hasn't been the same man since Todd died; and I know that I haven't been the ideal wife either. I don't blame him for drinking."

Pastor Cowley began to explore with Irene her involvement at Maple Avenue Church. "It is the least that I can do for the Lord. He has been so good to our family over the years. Todd has gone to be with the Lord. And I know now that the Lord wants me to serve his church as our Lord suffered for us. Todd's death was like a message from God; it was as if he were telling me that I owed him more than I was giving him."

Rather than responding directly to this pious expression of what seemed to him an immature faith, Pastor Cowley said, "I just don't know how you do it. I mean, where do you get the energy to do all that you do for Maple Avenue Church?"

At this point the direction of the conversation suddenly shifted. Irene disclosed that for five years her doctors had been prescribing tranquilizers for her because of persistent insomnia. All her life, Irene had battled a weight problem, following one diet after another, including diet pills. Since the diet pills acted as an "upper" for Irene, she used them to combat the grogginess she experienced from the prescription tranquilizer that her doctor ordered for her.

Pastor Cowley was beginning to see this as an overwhelming pastoral problem beyond his capacity alone. He was certain that religion was functioning as a two-edged sword for Irene. On the one hand, she perceived God as an angry autocrat who could and would punish people at will if he was not getting what he wanted out of them. On the other hand, God could perhaps be appeased by a combination of pious words about him and good deeds done for him.

Both George and Irene Matthews had been unsuccessful in dealing with their grief. Their religion was more yoke than comfort, more bullying club than healing hand. God appeared in their minds as a voracious beast, not a shepherding father.

Pastor Cowley was certain that their religious problems were the critical issues in the Matthews' lives. No matter. He was also certain that Irene and George both needed a psychiatric intervention which included an address to their drug problems—his with alcohol, hers with diet pills and tranquilizers. In his effort and anxiety to be helpful, Pastor Cowley had made the ill-fated suggestion, "Have you considered Pine Crest?"

Irene's sharply negative response had disconcerted him. Yet as he reflected further, he remained convinced that, though his approach had been blunt and abrupt, his assessment was valid and his recommendation appropriate.

QUESTIONS FOR FURTHER REFLECTION:

1. Comment on this suggestion about why Pastor Cowley's conversation with Irene Matthews broke down: "Religion is the private affair of the individual person. The pastor had no right to intervene on Irene's behalf until she requested his counsel."

2. When does pastoral care become pastoral counseling? When does pastoral counseling become pastoral intervention?

3. Is the notion that Christianity can take the form of a harmfully addictive religion really just a thinly veiled attack on a certain segment of the church commonly known as evangelicalism or fundamentalism?

4. Is it possible to love Jesus without "losing one's head," sacrificing one's rationality?

5. How would you distinguish between the "magic" which we have identified as an element of addictive religion and Christian faith, with its belief in the supernatural?

6. Do you think Irene needs a pastor or a psychiatrist?

7. Is the doctrine of "grace" really just a cushion to soften the harsh blows of reality?

8. What role does the acknowledgment of the inevitability of your own death play in your personal religious life?

9. "Most prayer is a quaint attempt to manipulate God and thus overcome the anxiety of being separated from the womb of 'Mother.'" Comment.

10. Religious activity is a tool of the demonic to forestall the coming kingdom. Comment.

Other Addictions

We have talked at length about love and addiction, alcoholism, and religious addiction. But of course there are many other addictions as well, all of them able to rob us of the very meaning and freedom we crave. Here are a few.

Workaholism

Terry comes home for supper at 6:30 P.M. He left for work at 7:30 that morning. While he belts down a gin and tonic, he surveys the latest from Wall Street. A buss of affection to satisfy his wife's need to relate to an adult, a pat on Terry, Jr.'s behind for the daily quota of quality time with the heir, and then it's time to eat. By 7:30 P.M. he's off again to a church meeting. Top it all off with a midnight review of tomorrow's agenda at the office.

Here is the profile of an addict. Terry drinks no more than he should, smokes only occasionally, jogs four times a week, and has survived his mid-life crisis without womanizing. But he is an addict nonetheless. And his wife supports the habit. She is long-suffering and understanding. She even brags about him at Bible study: "Oh, Terry is so busy lately; I just don't know how he can keep it up!"

The insidiousness of workaholism is its very acceptability. It is so middle-class. For so many men—and a growing number of women—their career controls them, not the other way around.

How does it happen? How does one's job become one's slave driver? It does so through a simple equation: achievement equals self-esteem. As we have seen, we are all driven at a deep level by a desire to gain absolute freedom and to avoid death, and many of us think that our careers will buy us the self-esteem we need to meet these internal objectives.

How we value ourselves is tied to what we make of ourselves, how much control we gain over others, how much money we make, how many promotional steps we take—on our way, all too often, to a coronary!

This sense of value begins to ingrain itself in our being when we are still children. "What are you going to be when you grow up?" The question implies, ever so subtly, that a child is not yet a being. My ticket to being a Somebody is my ability to master my chosen skill and profession.

Mastery and success are, of course, good ends in themselves; but as we internalize these values, we intensify and exaggerate their significance. Our self-esteem is at stake. After all, being frightened or failing is frowned upon. How can we be free when we are flunking? Walter Payton of the Chicago Bears was a picture of dejection after his team was blitzed by San Francisco in the '85 playoffs: "I will never forget this loss." Here you have it: the most successful running back in pro football history is still struggling for self-esteem. Failure is not to be tolerated. Winning is everything. Profit is the bottom line. And soon our careers have us by the neck. They control our relationships. They wreak havoc on our family life. They determine our mental and physical health. They indicate where we are on the socioeconomic scale.

But we claw at the rungs of the ladder because we want to be loved. And we believe that to get love we need to succeed. Success buys love. But the work addict tries too hard to get love. Terry gets lost on his climb. He never comes home anymore. Somewhere he loses the very thing he is looking for. He misses all the good that comes from authentic success. Given the pressures of society, men are probably more vulnerable than women. In hot pursuit of making it big, they tend to suppress their intuitive needs, their contemplative instincts, their creative urges, the spontaneous display of passion, joy, and surprise. Warm impulses toward wife and children are frozen out by the single-minded drive toward achievement.

And now the trap is sprung. Our workaholic begins to realize that his success is not really buying love and happiness after all—and in desperation he tries still harder to succeed. He is running on a treadmill.

Infrequent and erratic weekend trips with his family do not make up for the lost time, the emotional distancing, and the accumulated pain. Disappointed that the fantasy trip did not buy the love and stroking he expected, the workaholic retreats to the only world in which he finds comfort and solace. He rolls up his sleeves and returns to work. The corridor to freedom and happiness is transformed into a hall of horrors.

We have discussed some of the dynamics which explain a person's addiction to his (or her) career. Here are some of the symptoms. The workaholic

- toils long hours;
- brings work home;
- makes work the main topic of conversation;
- is more anxious and depressed during off hours than at work;
- never sees the job as done, or as done to his satisfaction;
- is rigid and compulsive while on the job;
- fails to "see" and "hear" his colleagues;
- is an individualist at work and not a team player;
- is always in a rush on the job (as if he were gulping drinks);
- is only momentarily pleased by rewards, promotions, bonuses, letters of commendation;
- sees all failures, all losses of opportunity, promotions, or contracts, as a personal reflection on his character (suicide is a danger here);
- gets deeper and deeper into his obsession;
- lives with the secret illusion that no one does it better than he does.

Interventions that work to alleviate the workaholic include a heart attack, the genuine threat of a divorce, marital or family therapy, and possibly a counseling group where personal issues are focused on. The workaholic needs to see that his work is a form of displacing other more personal concerns.

One might think that addiction to work is not as debilitating or destructive as addiction to alcohol. So-called type-A personalities suffering from chronic high blood pressure and cardiac problems due to career stress would strongly disagree. Families who must cope with a home made tense and miserable by workaholism would disagree. Employers who must respond to burnout in some of their best employees would disagree.

In a word, the success that comes with an effective career is not worth the sacrifice of good psycho/social and physical well being. The new generation of "yuppies" and university students is far too bent on success to notice the hazards and traps—which is too bad for them, and the rest of us.

Food

Hattie eats too much. Everyone knows that Hattie eats too much. It shows. Food addiction is harder to hide than the other addictions we've been discussing. Hattie herself may of course not visualize herself as fat. Her denial system takes care of that. Instead, she sees a thin person in the mirror of her mind (just as the sufferer from anorexia sees herself as grossly overweight). Addiction to food is stocked with its own complex cupboard of emotional dynamics. On the bottom shelf are a number of staples beside those we discussed in Chapter 1. What seems to stand out for the overeater is the deep fear that there will be no one left to love her. Her inordinate fear of abandonment is relieved ever so briefly just so long as she is eating. Her highest highs from eating come in the form of relief. It is in fact the only reliable way she can spell *relief*.

Never mind the guilt she has after the doctor, the nurse, and the maid have all pleaded with her to lose some pounds. Never mind the irrationality of sneaking meals between meals within sight of no one until it shows up all too clearly the next day. Never mind the principle of mind over matter, of willpower over emotion. The urge to eat without control or limitations or predictability is rooted deep down in the fear that no one will love her.

Every child fantasizes that his or her parents will always be there with their love. Every child is convinced that in time of trouble a parent will appear in the nick of time. Every child is anxious to know that his parent will always be there to do for him what he is not able to do for himself. But during this period of development, another person begins to emerge. It is the individual "I" who views himself as separate and free from the parent. He exudes freedom, space, and confidence about the great beyond. He begins to realize that he is a problem-solver and is responsible for taking charge of his life.

Most adults manage to resolve the tension between the dependent "I" and the free-wheeling one. Usually, it is a compromise. The alcohol addict denies all dependency and views himself as a limitless freewheeler until, of course, the crunch of defeat bludgeons him with the truth of his powerlessness and unmanageability. The overeater, on the other hand, never allows herself the challenge of stepping into her own independence. The water is too cold—and she retreats to the dependent self. Her anxiety, however, whispers the truth. Mother or father will not always be there, will not always come to the rescue, will not always be a near and present help in time of trouble. As the infant gropes and reaches and grabs for mother, so the overeater will take onto herself what has now become a visceral symbol—more food.

True, overeaters abuse food out of habit. And of course, it is a device to cope with all kinds of anxieties. It softens gloom, relieves boredom, relaxes tension, provides an emotional outlet, and creates a sugar high. But more than that, it symbolically takes the place of a mother's arms that reach out and under and through with love that will not fail.

Some overeaters simply enjoy food. Some are truly happy and well rounded emotionally as well as physically. They choose to overeat. They are not addicts. The food addict agonizes over his consumption. He knows he lies to himself when he convinces himself that he is thin. He knows that his eating habits are separating him from the life and love he craves; but he feels powerless to overcome his addiction.

It is difficult to tell a loved one that she must do something about her overeating. The situation is usually not dramatic or overtly traumatic. Nobody gets a traffic ticket for being overweight. Overweight people do not normally cause scenes in public facilities. The havoc they wreak in a home or at work is more subtle and less provocative. Still, the damage done is as dire in the long run as the damage done by the alcoholic.

Family relationships become phony. It is more pleasant to humor Hattie than to confront her. It is safest to laugh with her when she mocks her own obesity. It is simpler not to be in the kitchen when she does her thing. It is easier to avoid sex. Everyone in the family or at the office is a little tighter, less spontaneous, more guarded than they would otherwise be. Disgust pokes through now and then, and Hattie's old feelings of rejection and abandonment come alive. Embarassment chokes off joy in the family. Since it is easier to cater to Hattie than to embarrass her, she ultimately is left alone. This is the last nail in the coffin. Now she knows that she really *is* unlovable. The drama of denial can be played out just so long. Finally, the actors get tired and leave the show, leaving Hattie to herself.

Once the overeater hits bottom, the parallels between her and the recovering alcoholic are strikingly similar. Even as the dynamics which breed alcohol addiction are similar to those which lead to food addiction, so in the recovery process the dynamics are not only similar, they are exactly the same. Overeaters Anonymous and Alcoholics Anonymous are similar programs and are equally effective. All that is required is one's willingness to do something about his abuse of food. A sense of powerlessness and unmanageability are critically important.

Food addiction is one of the most difficult addictions to overcome—for obvious reasons. All the other addictions require abstinence, at least for a specified time. Abstinence is ordinarily the only way to any successful recovery. But obviously a person cannot abstain from eating.

It is critically important for the overeater to be with others who are in various stages of recovery. Overeaters Anonymous is an excellent example of a self-help group. It provides the necessary support and identification. The miracle of love begins to dawn. "It is possible that I *am* loved and that I can love others, too." Special diets, prescription aids to dieting, surgical stapling, and willpower are all bit players in the recovery scene. But the main characters are other overeaters who in their presence and compassion reach out to that fearful soul once lost on a sea of abandonment.

Fitness

A lot of us these days are fitness nuts. Part of "middle-age crazy" is spending half our life in running shorts and tennis shoes. Not an hour goes by but the hand creeps furtively over the abdomen to see if last night's tennis match has done some good. No such luck. So we run the extra mile, we pump the extra iron. Fitness becomes a life-style. America will never be fat again. No one sits on porches anymore with the neighbors. We're all on the run.

It may seem a bit irreverent to discuss fitness in the context of addiction. And even if it is an addiction, so what? Isn't it a positive addiction? It increases life expectancy to stay fit, eat right, and sleep well. In-shape people are beautiful people. Beautiful and shapely people get the job when all else is equal. No one hires a "grunt" over a "hunk." Beauty and fitness enhance the company image. If clothes don't make the man, the body certainly helps. What could possibly be harmful about a well-coordinated physical fitness program? Statistics prove that heart disease is trending downward in direct relationship to fewer people smoking. People feel better longer when they keep fit. Instead of groping feebly toward old age, people are striding forward in the picture of good health. Look at President Reagan: fitness pays.

Here are some of the hazards, symptoms, and possible outcomes of fitness addiction.

Initially, there are no bad side effects to keeping fit. Staying in shape *is* fun. Feeling healthy *is* one of life's gifts. But there are hazards. Loss of perspective is one. The urge to fitness is a problem when it makes a pastor routinely switch appointments, forget to show up at meetings, feign emergency hospital visits—all in order to get in some racquetball. It is a bit much to take two sets of workout clothes just in case one succeeds in scheduling another match later in the day. It is probably irresponsible to refuse a game of touch football with the kids on Saturday afternoon because of a tennis match. It is one thing to get up and out early and run the track; it is quite another to have a one-track mind.

Another hazard, common to most addictions, is the disruption it can create within the family. If Dad happens to be a racquetball freak, the whole family must tolerate his tardiness, his moodiness when he loses, his depression when he is injured, his windy reporting when he triumphs, and his wife's frustration when he is more interested in improving his serve than he is in his sex life. And there can come a point when the employer loses out too—to tardiness, story-swapping in the corridors, minds wandering to tonight's game. It is wonderful that some industries build their own private workout gym. But there are dangers in swapping the three-martini lunch for the ninety-minute fitness ritual. At least some business is conducted over the martinis.

A denial of death is the third hazard for the fitness addict. North American culture is hung up about death. Cosmetics and gilded caskets try to prettify the picture. Medical technology creates the illusion of life ever extendable. Modern-day Hezekiahs bargain with doctors for more days, more months, more years. We don't die; we are reincarnated. We don't die; we are resurrected. We don't die; our souls sleep. We won't die if we stay in shape. The promise of a long life without consideration of a quality life, of a life devoted to other people and a variety of interests, issues, and concerns is all that a fitness addict recognizes. It is pure egocentrism, a fixation on life alone rather than on a life *with* others and *for* others. It is navel-gazing at its worst: "How does my tummy sag?" becomes one of life's profounder problems.

What are the symptoms of fitness addiction? Here are some of them:

- an inordinate preoccupation with death
- an obsession with physical health
- hypochondriasis
- heightened anxiety during minor illness
- depression over minor injuries
- acute withdrawal when the game is cancelled
- "midnight madness"—our addict is out there at some ungodly hour exercising to compensate for time lost during illness or vacation
- "hide-the-shorts"—he is embarrassed by how much he plays; so he hides his workout clothes and they stay hidden until you smell that strange and not so wonderful aroma

- a preoccupation with self that is characterized by spending far too much money on fitness and not devoting enough quality time with the family

- a persistent and chronic fear of being physically unattractive.

This last symptom is worthy of further exploration. Our current culture is truly enamored with looking good, an obsession exploited of course by the media. Who wouldn't buy hardware from Frank Gifford or makeup from Christie Brinkley? Or the news from Dan Rather or Connie Chung? We internalize the values of external beauty. It is literally what's up front that counts. The fitness addict internalizes the value to an extreme so that he experiences undue anxiety about losing "it." And "it" is looking good. The sad scenario of Jack LaLanne towing row boats in a California Bay while shackled is a ludicrous parable of the malady.

But how do you know whether you are a fitness addict or just concerned about being fit? The telling is in the relationships you have and hold. Are your friends only buddies; are they people who are close to you only when you jog side by side? The person who is hooked simply has no interest in other persons as persons. Then it's time for an intervention.

Fitness addicts can benefit greatly from group therapy because here the person is invited to relate as a human being to other human beings, and not as a jock to another jock. Contrast the level of conversation in the locker room. It rarely gets much further than the number of touchdown passes Joe Montana threw in the Superbowl.

Our brief discussion of how work, food, and fitness can be addictive leads to one last statement. Here it is: "Whatever is true, whatever is noble, whatever is right, whatever is pure, whatever is lovely, whatever is admirable—if anything is excellent or praiseworthy—think about such things" (Philippians 4:8). To which we might add, think about these things and *practice* them. But not overmuch, lest they possess you and rob you of your precious freedom to choose. In their place, food, fitness, and work are lovely and true, admirable and excellent, noble and right. So are many other things: shopping, cleaning, doing crossword puzzles, driving, talking, listening—even writing books.

CHAPTER VII

On the Way
to Recovery and Freedom

We have looked in some detail at three expressions of addiction in human experience and briefly at three others. We might have chosen other examples, of course: the human race is a motley lot, and, particularly where economic success and technological development have brought increased leisure, we have added new twists to addiction, virtually turning it into an art form. One fad succeeds another in the continuous effort to stimulate the euphoric "highs" we naturally crave.

We thirst especially, it seems, for the edge of adventure in an age when science and technology have eliminated or reduced so many of the risks our ancestors lived with. Here is someone climbing a rock: "Look, Ma! No ropes!" There is someone leaping out of an airplane, colorful parachute unfolding against the blue sky. Someone else is swimming around Manhattan, or climbing its tallest skyscraper. These contemporary adventurers are engaged in passing expressions of a standing condition: the itch for euphoria and the urge to repeat those experiences—which leads to addiction.

Less glamorous are three prevalent addictions which receive considerable press coverage on the American scene: food,[1] work, and fitness. The dynamics of these addictions, as we have suggested, are similar to those of relationships, alcohol, and religion. The horror stories may vary in texture and tint, but the addictive process and function are readily observable and comparable.

Beyond all these specific manifestations of addiction, we have said, lies the reality of human existence. We may be a venerable lot, created only a little lower than the angels, but we are a vulnerable one too. The restless experience of life is one of constant and unfulfilled reaching or striving for a greater high until there is an inner surrender to the One who is for us, with us, and to us everything he was and is in Jesus Christ.

The mini-hells we experience are our own creation. We try to unseat the Creator from his throne, or to flee from his presence. Either way we lose. The gospel is good news counterpointing this fiasco. There is winning in losing; indeed, the only requirement for winning in this life is to lose. In biblical language, that means to die; and that includes all of us, because we all die. Becoming alive to this truth is what sets us free.

For some this process of surrender seems to happen almost naturally—no prodding, no pushing or pulling, no program. For many others, however, a structured program of recovery is necessary, because their habituation process has moved them from simple abuse to destructive compulsive behavior.

In either case, the secret of recovery from addiction and the freedom to make responsible choices are inseparably linked to *pain*. (We are not differentiating here between psychic and physical pain, although, as C. S. Lewis said, "it is easier to say 'My tooth is aching' than it is to say 'My heart is broken.'"[2])

We can trace the role of pain in turning people around by following the flawed footsteps of faith's finest heroes. David's repentance for his adultery with Bathsheba resulted from getting caught with his pants down. When Nathan hit him between the eyes with the story of the poor man and the rich man (2 Samuel 12), David saw the light. It was only after Paul was knocked off his horse and blinded to boot on the Damascus Road that he was ready to serve the Lord instead of continuing his fanatical pursuit of Christians. When Isaiah felt the burning coals on his lips, he overcame his self-doubts and became ready to answer the call of the Lord (Isaiah 6:1-8). Moses, awestruck by the presence of the Holy in a burning desert bush, took a little more persuading, but he, too, allowed himself to be sent. When the great fish belched Jonah up on the beach, the reluctant prophet turned toward Nineveh.

A pattern emerges. When people cross their personal threshold of tolerance to pain—the point at which they no longer feel capable or willing to withstand the anguish—they will react. Either they change their behavior pattern and turn to another source of comfort and relief from the stress of life; or they increase the dosage to intensify the experience that once brought them comfort and relief and then brought pain. Therein lies the mystery of recovery and the mystery of resistance to recovery.

Alcoholics Anonymous calls alcohol "cunning, baffling, and powerful."[3] In fact, alcoholic beverages are rather predictable and straightforward: they change the mood; they get a person drunk; and they work every time. It is the person who uses the drug that is unpredictable. Why does only 10 percent of the drinking population become addicted to the drug ethanol? What is it that enables the other 90 percent to moderate their drinking habits in the face of an emerging alcohol abuse problem? What causes a person to intensify use of a drug when it is beginning to cause serious life problems?

Addiction is a circuitous route from pain to pleasure to pain. Recovery begins when the addict's experience of pain is no longer covered by the experience of relief delivered by the chosen drug or obsession. Just as some people believe that dentists exist solely for taking care of toothaches (and serious ones at that) and so would never go to the dentist for a mere check-up, much less every six months, an addict is not going to consider a change of pattern for as long as the object of addiction is working to relieve stress. He or she will not consider entering recovery just because it is a good idea to check whether use has become abuse. "What works, works," is the addict's motto. As long as the booze numbs the pain, pour me another one. As long as the adulterous laision makes me feel good, let's keep meeting in cheap motels. As long as religion eases the guilt, practice it ever more obsessively. An addict does not see the light of day without experiencing the bleakness of night.

Human nature is prone to addiction, we have said. And this truth about addicts' resistance to recovery is a law of human nature: Persons do not grow, develop, mature, convert, or repent, until and unless an intervening confluence of events stops them just short of dead in their tracks.

On the one hand, addicts have a very low threshold of pain. It does not take much stress to drive them to the bottle, a sexual-relational encounter, or a religious ritual for a "fix." On the other hand, once fixated on that which alleviates the stress, they develop a high threshold of pain and are willing to suffer a great deal for the sake of the "fix." The recollection of the agony in the stress of life before the discovery of the magical fix makes the trauma of addiction and withdrawal fade by comparison. So, it's "hit me again, Sam" or "I'll say I'm working late; let's meet at 6:30." Masochistic symptoms emerge on an unconscious level: "Hurt me, so I can fix me" or "If you won't hurt me, I'll screw up in some way so that you have no choice but to hurt me." How do we explain the behavior of the alcoholic who is put in jail for driving while intoxicated, gets drunk on his release, goes home, beats his wife, and is jailed again for assault and battery? Many variables go into a decision to start the road to recovery, but the one indispensable factor is the addict's *will to recover*. He or she will turn to a recovery attitude when there has finally been enough hurt. A person's behavior change is in direct response to the pain experienced and the point at which he or she says "Enough!" This is usually not a rational or well-thought-out decision; it is a gut-wrenching, emotionally charged impulse that results in throwing in the towel of surrender. However, one person's crucible for conversion is another's excuse for continued abuse. Before we consider a specific strategy of recovery from addiction and an appropriation of the newfound freedom, we should look a little more deeply at the phenomenon of pain within the framework of recovery.

The experience of pain can be seen as a gift, in the sense of telling us that something is wrong. Protect an addict from pain, and you prolong the addiction process. Rescue an alcoholic from the "tank," pay the fine, clean up the mess, and you relieve that person from the consequences of abusive drinking and insure at least one more day in the sun of insanity.

Paul Brand, a missionary doctor in North Africa, talks about how leprosy causes its greatest harm by numbing the extremities and the warning system of pain.[4] The tragedy of leprosy may seem like a remote reality in the Western world, but there are millions of people in the developed world who suffer because they are numbed in another way—by alcoholism. And alcoholism and the use of other drugs are only the most obvious forms addiction takes. These people have numbed themselves, inoculated themselves against their painful experience of pain that could warn them to move in a new direction; but in their numbness they condemn themselves to perpetuate the addictive cycle.

The relation of pain to recovery is illuminated by some insightful remarks of C. S. Lewis. Human beings, he reminds us, are not merely imperfect creatures who have to be improved upon:

> We are, as Newman said, rebels who must lay down our arms. . . . To render back the will which we have so long claimed for our own, is in itself, whenever and however it is done, a grievous pain. . . . To surrender a self-will inflamed and swollen with years of usurpation is a kind of death.[5]

As long as the addiction process is going along swimmingly, why buck the current? Go with the flow. The deeper error and sin are, Lewis says, "the less their victim suspects their existence; they are masked evil." But pain is different. "Pain is unmasked, unmistakable evil. . . . Pain insists upon being attended to. God whispers to us in our pleasures, speaks in our conscience, but shouts in our pains." If, in Lewis's words, it takes a megaphone to rouse a deaf world, it takes a baseball bat to wallop a full-blown addict into consciousness. The game plan of the addict is to avoid and escape pain at any cost, usually through the pleasurable means of the broad way. Up against the crisis, he or she will turn tail in the opposite direction (conversion) or stubbornly "tough it out" (the chronic phase), donning the chemist's smock and delicately balancing the toxic intake in order to dull the senses one step short of deadening them. Unchecked, he or she will ultimately blow up the lab. As Jellinek puts it, "He will hit his 'bottom': go insane, die, or begin a recovery process."[6] Pain is indeed a terrible instrument, but it gives the victim of addiction the only opportunity he or she has for recovery. "It removes the veil," Lewis says. "It plants the flag of truth within the fortress of a rebel soul."[7] Not all addicts reach the point of unbearable, inescapable pain. And not all addicts who do reach that point recover. Most victims of a chronic addictive process do not recover,[8] primarily because of the irrational impulse to spit in the wind of the real world.

Having counseled over five hundred persons addicted to beverage alcohol, I can report that not one of those who experienced a recovery process did so without first crossing that personal threshold of pain, the point at which they were no longer willing to go through the revolving door of "detox-drunk-detox."

Given that harsh reality, a serious question arises for the family and other significant people in the addict's life. When do they cut the strings of affection and belonging? When do they "blow the whistle"? Do we let the addict go into free-fall and hit bottom at his or her own pace? Most recovery programs whose rate of recovery from alcohol addiction is excellent (e.g., the Johnson Institute in Minneapolis, The Meadows in Wickenburg, Arizona, Hazelden in Center City, Minnesota, St. Luke's Hospital in Phoenix) declare emphatically that it is the responsibility of a caring community to intervene at some point in the addictive process before the point of no return or the point at which irreparable damage is done to the immediate family or community. It is obviously irresponsible to cover for an alcoholic who works as an air traffic controller. It is also irresponsible for the believing community to turn a blind eye to the sick religious practices of its adherents. It is irresponsible for lovers to rely on an addictive relationship to sustain their life together.

It is clear that an intervention process which is appropriate for the alcohol addict will not ordinarily be suitable in the case of the person addicted to religion or relationships. The nature of these latter addictions limits the opportunity for the caring community to intervene. It is often simply none of their business, particularly when the problem is love and addiction.

The most the caring community can do to help victims of addictive relationships or religious experiences is to provide a ministry of presence and availability, particularly when their experience of pain has become so acute as to set in motion the recovery cycle. It is essential for us to share our observations of addictive behavior with them; but we have no ethical or ecclesiastical right to intervene in a situation that is not life-threatening. Pastoral care and church discipline must observe all the rules of love here, including patient compassion, tolerance, understanding, unconditional positive regard, and acceptance. The arms of patient compassion and tolerance can perhaps be extended a little longer in cases of religious or relational addiction than in cases of alcoholism, since there is generally more rationality available in non-chemically related addictions and thus more amenability to the confrontation encounter, and because alcoholics typically put themselves and others in more life-threatening situations than persons addicted to other experiences.

There is admittedly a fine line here, which must be carefully and deliberately drawn. The greater physical danger for too many people in allowing an alcoholic to hit bottom at his or her own speed does not in any way imply that the risks which non-chemically dependent addicts incur to themselves or others are insignificant. The emotional and spiritual damage may be even more severe in the lives of those addicted to religion or relationships. But they are also more readily within reach of recovery than are the chemically dependent persons.

If pain is the atmosphere necessary if the addict is to begin breathing freely, what are some indicators that the recovering person is in fact breathing freely and regularly without the aid of life-support equipment like compulsory psychotherapy or attendance at Alcoholics Anonymous?

Here are some indicators that a recovery process is well established. They are dynamic qualities experienced by fifty recovering alcohol addicts (who claimed to be sober for at least two years), observed over a six-year period.[9]

1. *Humility.* Humility in a recovering person is the ability to accept his or her own limits and to acknowledge these as gifts not liabilities. The person who manifests authentic humility has no need to apologize for weakness (making excuses and offering rationalizations) or to explain strength (displaying accomplishments and abilities).

2. *Gratitude.* An oft-repeated refrain in every Alcoholics Anonymous meeting is "My name is X and I am a grateful alcoholic." Gratitude is the expression of thanks for the lessons in living learned over the course of a lifetime of chronic addiction. "It took what it took to get me to this point where I am tonight. I am not what I want to be, I am not what I am going to be, but thank God I am not what I used to be." That person dynamically understands the providence of a higher power moving one over the sometimes rocky road from addiction to recovery and freedom.

3. *Acceptance.* The recovering person accepts his or her lot in life with a measure of celebration and renewed creativity. Harry Tiebout draws a distinction between submission and surrender in positing acceptance as a necessary quality in a recovering person. In submission, an individual accepts reality consciously but not unconsciously. Though the practical fact that one cannot at the moment lick reality is accepted, there is a feeling lurking in the unconscious that a day will come when one will be able to drink again. The struggle in fact is still on. On the other hand, in surrender, the ability to accept reality functions at the unconscious level. There is no residue of battle. Relaxation and freedom from strain and conflict ensue.[10]

4. *Surrender.* If the *act* of surrender is the acceptance of reality on the unconscious level, the emotional *state* of surrender is one in which there is a persistent capacity to accept reality. Accepting reality is not something passive. We are talking here about an active sense of reality as a place where one can live and function as a person, acknowledging responsibilities and feeling free to make that reality more livable for oneself and others. "There is no sense of 'must,' neither is there any sense of fatalism. With true unconscious surrender, the acceptance of reality means the individual can work in it, with it. The state of surrender is positive and creative."[11]

5. *"Exit Stage Right."* Thomas Szasz explains this well:

Powerful addictions . . . are actually both very difficult and very easy to overcome. Some people struggle vainly against such a habit for decades; others "decide" to stop and are done with it; and sometimes those who have long struggled in vain manage suddenly to rid themselves of the habit. How can we account for this? Not only is the pharmacology of the so-called addictive substance irrelevant to this riddle, but so is the personality of the so-called addict. What is relevant is whether the "addiction" is or is not a part of an internally significant dramatic production in which the "patient-victim" is the star. So long as it is, the person will find it difficult or impossible to give up the habit; whereas, once he has decided to close down this play and leave the stage he will find the grip of the habit broken and will "cure" himself of the "addiction" with surprising ease.[12]

6. *Diversity.* The recovering person is an eclectic, not a virtuoso. Like the versatile "good wife" of Proverbs 31, the recovering person does not burn himself or herself out on one project or singular adventure, but is willing to build a life on several pylons. Many addicts, unfortunately, get lost in a recovery program, confusing the blueprint for recovery with recovery. They are able to do little more than discuss the virtue of Alcoholics Anonymous; or they become God-obsessed, talking of little else than what the Lord is doing in their life; or they become convinced that they "will never love this way again"; or, if psychotherapy is meeting their need for recovery, they learn a whole new language of psychobabble, with which they bore everyone around them.

7. *Live and Let Live.* The recovering person minds his or her own business. In the words of AA, he or she refuses to "read someone else's inventory." Nothing is more tiresome in a relationship than constant unsolicited—and therefore unheeded—advice for every given situation. The person who lives and lets live is able to "go with the flow," in an unspoken, unmeasured, yet undoubted faith in the providence of God who is persistently moving history toward its ultimate goal.

The recovering person has come to terms not only with personal limitations but also with the anxiety always to do something about them. Alan Watts uses a picturesque image to illustrate that we cannot understand or control life's mysteries by trying to grasp them—any more than we can walk off with a river in a bucket. "If you try to capture running water in a bucket, it is clear that you do not understand it and that you will always be disappointed, for in the bucket, the water does not run. To 'have' running water you must let go of it and let it run."[13]

This is not to suggest that life is a free ride with no fares to pay. It is primarily a way of saying this: Mind your own business and let your neighbors mind theirs, even if that neighbor is the Lord God himself. This leads directly to another indicator of recovery.

8. *"Let Go and Let God."* Belief clings, faith lets go. Belief is the insistence that truth is what one would wish it to be. The believer seeks to force the truth into the shape of preconceived notions or ideas. Faith is an unreserved opening of the mind to the truth, whatever it might turn out to be. To discover Ultimate

Reality, the Absolute, the eternal Lord of Life, we must cease trying to grasp what cannot be grasped. "Have this mind in you which was also in Christ Jesus who did not count equality with God a thing to be grasped, but emptied himself, taking the form of a servant . . . " (Philippians 2:6-7).

The genius of AA's third step—"We made a decision to turn our will and life over to the care of God as we understood Him"—is potentially its fatal flaw. This is the surrender step, our release of the control switch of the future, when we entrust our life to Another. Alcoholics Anonymous often describes "letting go and letting God" in terms of a paradox: we do the legwork but trust that God will get us to the bus stop on time. Paul Tournier describes the true meaning of a religious experience as our coming to know God. "What matters is not our experiences but the fact that in them we have known the power of God's grace. . . . What is radically changed is the climate of our lives. If we still discover in ourselves strong or weak natural reactions, we shall see them as opportunities for new deliverance."[14]

The potential fatal flaw is that the person who takes this step may discover, define, or otherwise create his or her own personal religion, ignoring history. But this is just one more way to try to manipulate the environment. A god-in-a-box is one that I can call up at my convenience, rely on at will, surrender to when seemly. The so-called losers in the program of recovery are often those who continue to play God by developing their own version. Their surrender is no more than a temporary submission until the heat of confrontation is off; their conversion is actually a "lying low." Persons who are in authentic recovery show their colors at this point. Their surrender is sweet, because the God to whom they turn is one not of their own making but of their own choosing. And that choice is grounded in a sense of history. It is characterized not by resentment toward the religion of youth but by a clearer understanding and appreciation of the childlike faith to which one can return as an adult.

9. *Easy Does It.* Patience is the key. Recovering alcoholics experience a horrendous first year of sobriety. They have gone through the maze of the emotional high that accompanies the experience of discovering the outer limits of pain and the inner beginnings of surrender. It is like an emotional rollercoaster. Too many persons fail their personal programs of recovery because

they confuse seeing the light with walking in the light. The easiest thing for an addict to do is quit the addiction; the most difficult is to "stay quit." The first danger signal in a program of recovery is the too often repeated assertion: "I'll *never* do it again." The person in authentic recovery, on the other hand, avoids the pitfalls summed up in the acronym "HALT"—wallowing in the dangerous marshes of being too *h*ungry, too *a*ngry, too *l*onely, and too *t*ired. Nor does an authentically recovering person allow the experience of a relapse to become an excuse for giving up on recovery altogether. He or she stays with the daily program and does the legwork. "Action," not "reflection," is the key word. Sometimes it means "faking it until you can make it"— particularly in the spiritual dimensions of surrender and faith. It takes years to get to the point of chronic addiction; it will inevitably take time to live into consistent recovery.

A letter from Nadine Star, an 85-year-old woman in Kentucky, puts the insight of "easy does it" in vivid terms. If she could live life over again, she says, she would:

> Dare to make more mistakes next time. I'd relax. I would limber up. I would be sillier than I have been this trip. I would take fewer things seriously. I would take more chances. I'd climb more mountains and swim more rivers. I'd eat more ice cream and less beans. I would perhaps have more actual troubles but I'd have fewer imaginary ones.
>
> You see, I'm one of those people who live sensibly and sanely hour after hour, day after day. Oh, I've had my moments, and if I had it to do over again, I'd have more of them. In fact, I'd try to have nothing else, just moments one after another instead of living so many years ahead of each day. I've been one of those persons who never goes anywhere without a thermometer, a hot water bottle, a rain coat, and a parachute. If I had to do it again, I would travel lighter than I have.
>
> If I had my life to live over, I'd start barefoot earlier in the Spring and stay that way later in the Fall. I'd go to more dances; I'd ride more merry-go-rounds; I'd pick more daisies.

10. *One Day At a Time.* There is a wall plaque in my office given to me by a recovering person. The words on it have been credited to numerous authors. We quote them here as an anonymous contribution to our understanding of recovery:

There are two days in every week about which we should not worry; two days which should be kept free from fear and apprehension.

One of these days is *Yesterday,* with its mistakes and cares, its faults and blindness, its aches and pains. Yesterday has passed forever beyond our control. All the money in the world cannot bring back yesterday; we cannot undo a single act we performed; we cannot erase a single word said. Yesterday is gone.

The other day we should not worry about is *Tomorrow,* with its possible burdens, its large promise, and poor performance. Tomorrow is also beyond our immediate control. Tomorrow's sun will rise either in splendor or behind a mask of clouds; but it will rise. Until it does we have no stake in tomorrow, for it is yet unborn.

This leaves only one day. *Today.* Any man can fight the battle of just one day. It is only when you and I have the burden in those two awful eternities, *Yesterday* and *Tomorrow,* that we break down.

It is not the experience of *Today* that drives men mad—it is the remorse or bitterness for something which happened yesterday and the dread of what tomorrow may bring.

Let us, therefore, live but one day at a time.

Recovering persons are learning, though they have not yet fully learned, the secret of living one day at a time.

11. *Grace-full.* The person successfully moving from addiction toward freedom is one sweetened by the awesome reality of God's grace, as the mystery of the gospel unfolds itself. Robert F. Capon sets the full implication of this gospel in sharp relief against the legalistic notion that we finally have to save ourselves:

The salt mine is closed. You are dead to the law by the body of Christ. This means that it is not only you who are dead and beyond the orbit of blame; but God too. God Himself, the Supreme Lawgiver, Blamefixer, and Guiltspreader, has died to the whole sorry business in the death of Jesus. . . . There is therefore no condemnation. It does not matter what the universe thinks. It does not matter what other people think. It does not matter what you think. It does not even matter what God thinks because God has said that he was not going to think about it anymore. All He thinks now is Jesus, Jesus, Jesus; and Jesus is now all your life. You are therefore free.[15]

Recovering persons are free on the basis of grace, not by discovering a secret but because God has discovered them, made his way into their heart. This has nothing to do with finding a great new technique, a super gimmick, a better way to pull strings, but because grace was no longer resistible. The gates of his inner hell could no longer prevail against the rush of grace.

Søren Kierkegaard described this free person as the "knight of faith." Though he claimed never to have seen a knight of faith, he did not deny that every other person may be such a knight.

> I examine him from head to foot, hoping to discover a chink through which the infinite can peer. But No! He is completely solid. How does he walk? Firmly. He belongs wholly to the finite; he belongs altogether to the earth. No trace of exquisite exclusiveness. He takes pleasure in all things. He does his job thoroughly. He goes to church but you could not distinguish him from the rest of the congregation. His heart rejoices over everything he sees; the crowds, the new omnibuses, the sounds. In the evening he smokes his pipe, and to see him you would swear that he was the butcher, vegetating in the evening twilight. He is free from cares as any ne'er do well, but every moment of his life he purchases his leisure at the highest price; for he makes not the least movement except by virtue of the absurd. This man is making at every moment the movement of infinity. He knows the blessedness of infinity; he has known the pain of forsaking everything in the world that was not dear to him; and yet the task of the finite is as pleasing to him as if he had never known anything higher for he remains in the finite.[16]

Kierkegaard's knight of faith has one foot in the finite and the other in the Infinite. The perspective from that vantage point is the freedom to see things as they are with the blessed assurance of seeing things as they should and will be. It is Ecclesiastes turned on its head: the emptiness and "vanity" of the experience described by the Old Testament Preacher are filled in a life hidden in Christ.

But how does the addict get to that point? What steps can be taken from pain toward recovery and freedom? The twelve steps of Alcoholics Anonymous have been a godsend for thousands of recovering alcoholics. Their familiar claim holds water: "Rarely have we seen a person fail who had thoroughly followed our path. . . . If you have decided you want what we have and are willing to go to any length to get it, you are ready to take certain steps."[17]

Capon writes of how our freedom in the grace of Jesus Christ is freedom from the bondage to religious ritual:

The ineffectuality of such rituals is not the real root of their silliness. They're foolish not because they're the wrong tool for the job of jimmying the universe into line but because the job has already been done by Jesus. Indeed, thank God they *are* the wrong tool: if the likes of us really had the power necessary to straighten out the world, we'd make it a bigger mess than it is. . . .

In the long run Christianity is not a religion. While it uses the forms of religion—while it has observances, days and seasons that seem to be intended to fix up our relationship with God and the universe—it is in fact the announcement of the end of any need for such influencing at all. It is the proclamation of the gospel that God has fixed up everything himself and it is an invitation to believe that incredibly cheerful piece of good news.[18]

And with that, the addict is home free. And so are all of us.

Notes

Preface

1. Kurt Vonnegut, *Deadeye Dick* (New York: Delacorte Press, 1982), p. 142.

Chapter One

1. *Alcoholics Anonymous* (New York: World Services Publications, 1955), *passim.*
2. B. Zilbergeld, *The Shrinking of America* (New York: Little Brown, 1983), *passim.*
3. See William Glasser, *Positive Addiction* (New York: Harper and Row, 1978).

Chapter Two

1. C. S. Lewis, *Perelandra* (New York: Macmillan, 1944), p. 48.
2. The phrase Paul uses in verse 8 is variously translated as "covetousness" (RSV), "selfish desires" (TEV), "covetous desire" (NIV).
3. St. Augustine, *The Confessions of St. Augustine* (New York: Washington Square Press, 1951), p. 37.
4. *Ibid.,* p. 2.
5. Paul Tournier, *Guilt and Grace* (New York: Harper and Row, 1957).
6. Henry Stob, *Ethical Reflections* (Grand Rapids: Eerdmans, 1978), p. 176.
7. Herb Goldberg, *The Hazards of Being MALE* (New York: Nash Publishing, 1976), p. 27.
8. Erich Fromm, *Escape From Freedom* (New York: Holt, Rinehart, and Winston, 1965), p. 44.
9. Robert Gould, *Transformations* (New York: Simon and Schuster, 1978), p. 27.
10. John Steinbeck, *East of Eden* (New York: Viking Press, 1952), p. 346.

11. Fromm, *op. cit.*, p. 50.

12. Alan Watts, *The Wisdom of Insecurity* (Toronto: Vintage Press, 1951), p. 20.

13. *Ibid.*

14. Ray S. Anderson, *On Being Human* (Grand Rapids: Eerdmans, 1983), p. 82.

15. Fromm, *op. cit.*, p. 124.

16. *Ibid.*

17. Robert F. Capon, *The Youngest Day* (New York: Harper and Row, 1983), p. 23.

18. Peter DeVries, *Slouching Towards Kalamazoo* (Boston: Little Brown, 1983), p. 117.

19. C. S. Lewis, *The Problem of Pain* (New York: Macmillan, 1940), p. 91.

20. S. Kierkegaard, *The Sickness Unto Death* (New York: Anchor, 1954), p. 181.

21. *Alcoholics Anonymous*, p. 62.

22. Paul Tillich, *Systematic Theology*, Vol. I (Chicago: University of Chicago Press, 1957), p. 51.

23. Reinhold Niebuhr, *The Nature and Destiny of Man*, Vol. I (New York: Scribners, 1941), pp. 233-34.

24. *Ibid.*, p. 235.

25. Anderson, *op. cit.*, p. 94.

26. Helmut Thielicke, *Living With Death* (Grand Rapids: Eerdmans, 1983), p. xi.

27. *Ibid.*, p. 26.

28. Ernest Becker, *The Denial of Death* (New York: Macmillan, 1973), p. ix.

29. William James, *The Varieties of Religious Experience: A Study in Human Nature* (New York: Longmans Green & Co., 1925), p. 121.

30. *Ibid.*, p. 119.

31. *Ibid.*

32. Becker, *op. cit.*, p. 27.

33. *Ibid.*, p. 66.

Chapter Three

1. Kurt Vonnegut, *Breakfast of Champions* (New York: Delacorte Press, 1974), p. 210.

2. Quoted by Charles Williams, in *The Figure of Beatrice* (London: Faber & Faber, 1943), p. 68.

3. E.g., by Stanton Peele (with Archie Brodsky), *Love and Addiction* (New York: New American Library, 1976).

4. D. H. Lawrence, *Women in Love* (Penguin edition, 1960), p. 37.

5. Sheila Graham and Gerold Frank, *Beloved Infidel* (New York: Henry Holt, 1958).

6. Fromm, *The Art of Loving* (New York: Harper and Row, 1956), p. 19.

7. Peele, *op. cit.*, p. 83.

8. Fritz Perls, *Gestalt Therapy Verbatim* (Salt Lake City: Real People Press, 1967), p. 74.

9. Sheldon Van Auken, *A Severe Mercy* (New York: Harper and Row, 1973), pp. 127-50.

Chapter Four

1. Stanton Peele, "The Human Side of Addiction," *The US Journal of Alcohol Studies* (June 1981), p. 7.

2. *Ibid.*

3. Donald Goodwin, *Is Alcoholism Hereditary?* (New York: Oxford University Press, 1976).

4. David Ohlms, *The Disease Concept of Alcoholism* (Belleville, Ill.: Gary Whiteaker, 1983).

5. J. Milam and K. Ketchem, *Under the Influence: A Guide to the Myths and Realities of Alcoholism* (Seattle, Wash.: Madrona Publishers, 1981), and R. D. Myers and C. D. Melchior, "Alcohol Drinking: Abnormal Intake Caused by Tetrahydropapaveroline in Brain," *Science* 196 (1977), 554-56.

6. Sobell, Sobell, and Pattison, *Emerging Concepts of Alcoholism* (New York: Springer, 1977), *passim.*

7. Holmes, "Evangelicals and Experience," in *The Reformed Journal* (Sept. 1977).

8. Stanton Peele, *Love and Addiction*, p. 27.

9. James R. Milan, *The Emerging Concept of Alcoholism* (Kirkland, Wash.: Alcoholism Center Associates Press, 1972), p. 3.

10. H. Wallgren and H. Burz, *Actions of Alcohol* (New York: Elsevier, 1970), p. 37.

11. Cf. Kittel (ed.), *Theological Dictionary of the New Testament* (Grand Rapids: Eerdmans, 1962), II, 144.

12. Marlin Jeschke, *Disciplining the Brother* (Scottsdale, Pa.: Herald, 1972), p. 38.

13. Emil Brunner, *The Divine Imperative* (Philadelphia: Westminster, 1947), pp. 558-59.

14. Karl Barth, *The Faith of the Church* (New York: Meridian, 1958), pp. 157-58.

15. Lewis B. Smedes, *Love Within Limits* (Grand Rapids: Eerdmans, 1978), p. 18.

16. This is a modification of an intervention technique originated by the Johnson Institute, St. Paul, Minnesota.

17. The two-step disciplinary process ("silent censure" and "excommunication") seems to me to be unwarranted by both Scripture and sound intervention procedures. This final step of excommunication ought not to be administered without comparable decisions by both family members and employer.

Chapter Five

1. William James, *The Varieties of Religious Experience*, p. 387.

2. Thomas Wolfe, *Look Homeward, Angel* (New York: Scribners, 1929), p. 411.

3. Howard Clinebell, *Understanding and Counselling the Alcoholic* (New York: Abingdon, 1956), p. 145.

4. "The Bill W. and Carl Jung Correspondence," in *Grapevine*, January 1963.

5. Clinebell, *op. cit.,* p. 17.

6. J. B. Phillips, *Your God Is Too Small* (New York: Macmillan, 1961), p. 34.

7. Fromm, *Escape from Freedom,* pp. 82-86.

8. David Roberts, *Psychotherapy and a Christian View of Man* (New York: Scribners, 1950), pp. 112-13.

9. Harry Tiebout, "Conversion as a Psychological Phenomenon," in *The American Journal of Psychiatry,* June 1944.

10. Sigmund Freud, *The Future of an Illusion,* tr. J. Strachey (New York: Norton, 1961), p. 24.

11. E. Jones, *The Life and Work of Sigmund Freud* (New York: Double-day Anchor, 1963), p. 198.

12. Hans Küng, *Freud and the Problem of God* (New Haven: Yale University Press, 1979), p. 88.

13. Summarized in *The Road to H* (New York: Doubleday, 1966).

14. Stanton Peele, "Addiction: The Analgesic Experience," *Human Nature,* I, 9 (1978), 66.

15. Karl Barth, *Church Dogmatics,* I/2 (Edinburgh: T. & T. Clark, 1936), p. 280.

16. *Alcoholics Anonymous,* p. 37.

17. Paul Tillich, *The Courage to Be* (New York: Yale University Press, 1952), p. 72.

18. Paul Tillich, *Systematic Theology,* I, 13.

19. Frederick Buechner, *Wishful Thinking* (New York: Harper and Row, 1979), p. 27.

20. Gordon Allport, *The Individual and His Religion* (New York: Macmillan, 1950), pp. 57-74.

21. Søren Kierkegaard, *The Sickness Unto Death* (New York: Anchor, 1954), p. 181.

22. Quoted by Wayne Oates, *When Religion Gets Sick* (New York: Macmillan, 1970), p. 46.

23. Earl Jabaay, *The Kingdom of Self* (Plainfield, N.J.: Logos, 1974), *passim.*

24. E. Mansell Pattison, *The Effects of Religious Cultural Values Upon Personality Psychodynamics* (Berkeley: American Association for the Advancement of Science, 1965), p. 105.

25. Oates, *op. cit.,* p. 125.

26. Paul Tournier, *A Doctor's Casebook in the Light of the Bible* (New York: Harper and Row, 1960), p. 118.

27. C. G. Jung, *Psychology and Religion: West and East,* Volume III of Collected Works English translation (Stubenausgabe: Olten, 1971), p. 148.

Chapter Seven

1. Novelist Peter DeVries calls gluttony "an emotional escape, a sign that something is eating us." *Slouching Towards Kalamazoo* (Boston: Little, Brown, 1983), p. 42.

2. C. S. Lewis, *The Problem of Pain* (New York: Macmillan, 1940), p. 156.

3. *Alcoholics Anonymous,* p. 55.

4. Dorothy Clarke Wilson, *Ten Fingers for God, a Biography of Paul Brand* (New York: Macmillan, 1972), p. 174.

5. C. S. Lewis, *The Problem of Pain,* pp. 91-93.

6. E. M. Jellinek, *The Disease Concept of Alcoholism* (New York: Harper and Row, 1951), p. 24.

7. C. S. Lewis, *The Problem of Pain,* p. 95.

8. Calvary Rehabilitation Center in Phoenix, Arizona, reports a recovery rate of 1 in 15 for those who maintain their sobriety one year or more upon completing the program of recovery.

9. This survey was taken between 1973 and 1979 at Calvary Rehabilitation Center, Phoenix, Arizona.

10. Harry M. Tiebout, *The Act of Surrender in The Therapeutic Process* (New York: National Council on Alcoholism, 1965), p. 8.

11. *Ibid.,* p. 9.

12. Thomas Szasz, *The Second Sin* (New York: Doubleday, 1974), p. 72.

13. Alan Watts, *The Wisdom of Insecurity* (New York: Random House, 1968), p. 24.

14. Paul Tournier, *The Strong and the Weak* (Philadelphia: Westminster, 1963), p. 248.

15. Robert F. Capon, *Between Noon and Three: A Parable of Romance, Law, and the Outrage of Grace* (New York: Harper and Row, 1982), p. 118.

16. Søren Kierkegaard, *Fear and Trembling,* tr. Robert Payne (Princeton, N.J.: Princeton University Press, 1944), p. 48.

17. *Alcoholics Anonymous,* p. 58.

18. Capon, *The Youngest Day,* p. 136.

Steps to Healthy Living

An addictive abusive behavior can be defined as any activity—such as the use of alcohol, drugs, sexual activity, religion, day-dreaming, excessive work or activity, or people—that provides a temporary "fix" from emotional or physical discomfort; it is not a permanent resolution of the discomfort. The consequences of using such behavior, when continued over any length of time, whether periodic or on-going, will always be a significant deterioration in our mental, physical, spiritual, and social well-being. It is a serious disorder which directly and indirectly affects not only the life of the user but also those around him.

For those who have a desire to change their unhealthy life-style and to quit abusing people, places, and things, and are willing to be honest with themselves and others, Alcoholics Anonymous has developed twelve steps toward recovery. Those who follow the steps have a 75 percent chance of recovering from their addictive behavior. The 25 percent who don't make it are those who insist on "doing it their own way" rather than a healthy way. The questions in this Appendix, developed by the Calvary Rehabilitation Center of Phoenix, Arizona, may help you to work through the first seven steps.

Most addictive self-abusive people have a strong emotional desire to change their life-style during the early stage of recovery. The emotion behind this desire is fear, but, like all fear, it tends to become less noticeable or felt the longer we stay away from its cause, which is using these quick fixes to avoid the discomfort.

To stop using these behaviors is an absolute necessity for recovery, but it is not enough by itself to sustain a life of peace, serenity, joy, and love. Simply quitting them without making any other changes in your life-style may, in fact, turn out to be "pure hell."

Therefore, the longer we remain convinced of our powerlessness and unmanageability at the feeling level, the better our chances of following through. The following questions are offered with the hope that they might help you to accept, at the feeling level, your powerlessness over people, places, and things, and the unmanageability of your life. We urge you to write the answers down on paper, even though you may feel uncomfortable doing so. Unless you are willing to take an honest, detailed look at what abusing people, places, and things has done to your life, there is *no* chance you can sustain a healthy, responsible life-style. If we don't clearly see and feel how bad the problem is, we won't feel the need to do anything about it.

Before beginning, it is important that you understand that answering these questions is not a confession of character defects or faults, it is simply an honest look at how your addictive behavior has harmed your life and that of others.

Second, it is important to choose a good and faithful friend or wise and understanding pastor or counselor with whom you can share your answers. *Do not* do these written steps without the loving support and attention of this loyal friend or counselor. Be ready to tell this person who you are, step by step. Do not do this trip alone, or it will simply be one more exaggerated attempt to "do it yourself."

When writing out your answers, try to keep in mind the following points:

1. Being honest about the seriousness of your addictive life-style will give you a better chance of recovery—75 percent, if you are willing to follow the twelve steps provided by A.A.

2. Fear alone won't help you to maintain a healthier life-style.

3. You have a better chance of following through and sustaining a healthy life-style the longer you remain emotionally convinced of your powerlessness and unmanageablility.

4. Your addicted behavior affects your life and that of others.

5. Writing out your answers to the questions will help you to feel the need to do something about your addiction.

6. This is simply an honest look at what your addiction behaviors have done to you and others, not a confession of faults.

7. Remember, you will be sharing this with a trustworthy friend.

Do not worry about your spelling, punctuation, or writing skill. This is a self test; you will do your own "grading." Answer all questions very thoroughly, citing specific incidents and approximate dates or ages, etc. Use more paper if necessary.

STEP 1

1. Describe your childhood homelife. How would you describe
   your relationship with the important people in your life? Be
   thorough, describe each specific relationship.

2. Share two of your most pleasant and two of the most painful experiences in your life. Be specific; describe incidents.

3. When did you first use your addictive abusive behavior to fix yourself from a feeling of discomfort? What happened? How did you feel emotionally?

4. When did you first realize that you couldn't stop your addictive abusive behavior once you started? What happened? (For example, did you ever drink or use more than you planned?) How did you feel emotionally about it when it was over?

5. Other people began telling you they thought you were overdoing it. Who were they? When did that happen? Describe each specific incident and tell how you felt emotionally about it then and how you feel emotionally about it now.

6. When did you experience your first memory blackout? What did others say that you did during that time? How did you feel emotionally?

7. When did you first see your addictive abusive behavior as a serious problem? What happened? How did you feel emotionally?

8. What did you abuse (alcohol, drugs, sexual activity, religion, daydreaming, excessive work or activity, or people)? How did you feel emotionally when you were not abusing these things? What did you do?

At some point in your life you became addicted, hooked or powerless over people, places, and things. It is usually a slow process. Explore how it happened by answering the following questions as accurately as possible and you will discover how your addictive abusive behavior has affected you, how it has caused you to compromise your *basic values*. Write down how you feel about that right now.

9. Somewhere along the way your desire to fix your discomfort with addictive abusive behavior began interfering with things in your life. How did your constant attempts to do so interfere with social or recreational activities (hobbies, sports, dating, vacations, picnics, etc.)?

10. Did you increase the amount of your abuse during times of stress or discomfort resulting from job, family, or personal problems? Give detailed examples of each.

11. Tell specifically how your addictive abusive behaviors progressively became more and more frequent from the time you began using to the present; noting when your tolerance increased; when quantity and frequency increased; when you began behaving abusively in secret where others could not see; and when you began hiding your booze and drugs.

You used people, places, and things, and then "they started using you." That's when you started to *lose control* and you will *never* be able to control their use again. You began to abuse when you really didn't want to. Give examples by answering the following questions to help you see how this uncontrolled use damaged your's and others' lives.

12. How did your addictive abusive behavior gain control and cause harmful family consequences? Tell about: (1) broken promises to self or others; (2) embarrassing behavior in front of family; (3) physical abuse of yourself and other members of your family. Be specific. How did you *feel* emotionally about those things after each incident; how do you feel emotionally about them now?

13. How much time of undivided attention do you or did you spend with your spouse, children, parents, etc.? How do you feel emotionally about that right *now*?

14. Tell how your addictive abusive behaviors gained control and caused you *legal* problems—such as traffic incidents, arrests, lawsuits, or divorce. Give specific detailed examples of each. How do you *feel* emotionally about that now?

15. Tell how your addictive abusive behaviors caused you *social* problems, like the loss of friends, inability to perform sexually, unreasonable demands. Tell how it interfered with your sexual relationships. How do you feel emotionally about that now?

16. Tell how your addictive abusive behavior caused you *job* problems, like being absent from work, the loss of promotions, threats of being fired if you didn't stop. What happened when you were unable to perform well at work?

17. Tell how your addictive abusive behavior caused you to blame or *accuse others* for your problems. List what special problems you have used for excuses. What was your favorite excuse? Give specific detailed examples. How do you *feel* emotionally about that now?

18. Make three columns. In the first, list the uncomfortable emotional feelings you have tried to manage with your addictive abusive behavior. In column 2, list the ways that you managed these feelings without these abusive behaviors. *Be specific.* State in column 3 how well any of these methods worked.

19. Think about how you have ignored or rejected your religious and moral values when you behaved in addictive abusive ways; then list below some of the things that you did while abusing that you *feel* most guilty about now.

20. Why did you decide to seek help at this time? In what way is this different than before? What lengths are you willing to go to? List each length you are willing to go to and note which ones you feel will be the most difficult.

STEP 2

The second step to healthful living involves coming to the realization that there is "a Power greater than ourselves" that "could restore us to sanity." We have recognized that we cannot cure our addictive abusive behavior by ourselves, but we must now realize and believe that a Higher Power can do just that. These next questions should help you identify that Higher Power and to come to an awareness of your relationship with him.

1. Draw a picture of your Higher Power as you understand him; in particular, concentrate on the face of your Higher Power. Then write a paragraph about your drawing.

2. Describe the personality of God as you understand him.

3. Describe your *earliest* spiritual experience. What was it like?

4. Who in your family (parent, grandparent, etc.) reminds you of God?

5. If you were God, how would you change the world, and what would you do with a person such as yourself?

6. What qualities do you think a Higher Power *should* have? How is that different from the qualities you think a Higher Power *does* have?

7. Where did you get your notions, ideas, and beliefs about God (what sources or teachers)? Who or what taught you about God in the first place, and how did you receive such teachings?

8. If God were to return you to sanity, how would you like to be different? What does "sanity" mean to you?

9. List any resentments that you have toward God. When did they begin, and how did they begin? Could you forgive God?

10. If you had an interview with God, what would you ask him? What would you want to know about your standing with him? What would you tell him?

11. List specific incidents of how you have succeeded or failed to stay sober or clean trying on your own power.

12. What about Jesus? What do you believe about him? Do you believe that he can heal you?

If you choose to do so, read the following Scripture passages as you consider your answers to the above questions, and then discuss them with your friend or pastor: Psalms 19, 23, 27, 32, 51, 103, 139; John 3, 9, 10, 14.

The following scale is not meant to measure your spiritual well-being, but is designed to nudge you into the direction of the spiritual realm. For each of the following statements write the number which best indicates the extent of your agreement or disagreement as it describes your personal experience:

1 = Strongly Agree	4 = Disagree
2 = Moderately Agree	5 = Moderately Disagree
3 = Agree	6 = Strongly Disagree

1. I don't find much satisfaction in private prayer with God. ____
2. I don't know who I am, where I came from, or where I'm going. ____
3. I believe that God loves me and cares about me. ____
4. I feel that life is a positive experience. ____
5. I believe that God is impersonal and not interested in my daily situations. ____
6. I feel unsettled about my future. ____
7. I have a personally meaningful relationship with God. ____
8. I feel very fulfilled and satisfied with life. ____
9. I don't get much personal strength and support from my God. ____
10. I feel a sense of well-being about the direction my life is headed in. ____
11. I believe that God is concerned about my problems. ____
12. I don't enjoy much about life. ____
13. I don't have a personally satisfying relationship with God. ____
14. I feel good about life. ____
15. My relationship with God helps me not to feel lonely. ____
16. I feel that life is full of conflict and unhappiness. ____
17. I feel most fulfilled when I'm in close communion with God. ____
18. Life doesn't have much meaning. ____
19. My relationship with God contributed to my sense of well-being. ____
20. I believe there is some real purpose for my life. ____

STEP 3

While it is important to acknowledge that there is a Higher Power who can restore your sanity, it is also necessary to turn your will and life over to the care of God—however you understand him. This is the third step to healthful living. Discuss these questions with a pastor or counselor, and be prepared to make a decision to surrender your will to God.

1. What does "surrender" mean to you? (Look it up in a dictionary if necessary, then apply its meanings to yourself.)

2. List any specific fears that you have about surrendering your will and life to God.

3. What will it cost you to turn your will and life over to the care of God? What will be the rewards or benefits?

4. Write down the words you will use for your decision to trust God with your will and life.

5. Write a letter to God. Include in that letter at least these items:
   a. What you are thankful for.
   b. What you are sorry for.
   c. What you are angry about with him.
   d. What you need to forgive him for.
   e. What you need from him.
   f. What you want from him.
   g. What you hope to do to express your love for him.

Further Scripture passages that you may want to study are: John 3:16; Romans 10:9; 12:1, 2; 1 John 4:15.

STEP 4: A MORAL INVENTORY

If you have honestly answered the above questions, and have made a decision to turn your will and life over to God, you are ready for the next step. In order to live a healthy life, you must first recognize what is unhealthy in your present life. This marks the beginning of a new way of life. It means that you will begin to take a realistic assessment of yourself, to begin to learn more about yourself.

To be most successful in discovering your true self, you need to be searching, fearless, and moral. That is, as you answer these questions, ask yourself if you are really digging into your own self-awareness and describing your behavior as it really is. Second, be fearless; it takes courage to face yourself in terms of what has really been going on in your life. Third, take a good look at the "good/bad" implications of your behavior. How does it size up with your own values?

It is necessary to take a searching, fearless, and moral inventory, but don't be moralistic. You know your behavior has good and bad aspects; that is a fact of life. Look at it; own your own behavior. But don't punish yourself. Your goal is to know yourself and to accept yourself, for only then can you begin to change and grow.

This step is a simple, direct beginning to an on-going task of life—a direction to walk toward self-awareness, a way to go today and each day from now on. The moral inventory becomes a way of life based on the courage to be honest with ourselves.

You may experience some distress while writing your answers to these questions. This is normal. You may find yourself growing resentful, becoming depressed, feeling guilty, afraid of failure. You may find yourself "putting it off until tomorrow." Share these thoughts and feelings with your friend or pastor, and make what you discover a part of your inventory.

This may well be the most courageous act of your life. You need help and support, so don't be afraid to ask for it. Don't try to do this on your own.

Moral Inventory

Before you begin, consider the following definition: Resentment means having a desire to get even, which is expressed by anger, temper tantrums, rages, sulks, and other immature ways of responding to hurt or fear of being hurt. Resentful people hang onto angry feelings: about our families; about how we live and where and when. Hanging onto bad feelings can really make us miserable. Resentments are always good excuses for our irresponsible behavior.

1. List and number each resentment you have had against people, places, or things. Start with childhood resentments, then list teenage resentments, then those you have had or do have as an adult.

2. What caused the resentment? (Describe the incident.)

3. What about you was threatened by this resentment and its cause? (Was it physical well-being, self-esteem, financial well-being, approval of others, or a relationship?)

Remember, this is *your* inventory—not other peoples'. Put out of your mind the wrongs others have done you. Look once again, carefully, at each resentment. Disregard the other person, place, or thing entirely. As you review each resentment, look only at your own behavior. Where were you selfish, dishonest, self-seeking, or frightened? Where were you to blame? Write your answer to the following question.

4. What were your mistakes? How did you react to the situation?

Sometimes we're afraid of specific things—that someone will reject us, that a plan won't work, that someone will find us out—and sometimes we're afraid in some vague, general way that we are bound to fail, that nothing will work out, that everything is going wrong.

1. List what you were and are afraid of (person, place, or thing).

2. What caused the fear?

3. What was threatening you?

4. Now review your list of fears one by one. Looking only at yourself and your behavior, list, after each fear, whether:
   a. I relied too much on myself.
   b. I relied too much on others.
   c. I was selfish.
   d. I was self-centered.
   e. I was cocky.
   f. I was self-willed (wanting my own way).

Remember, if you have honestly turned your will and life over to God, you can ask him to remove your fear and to direct your attention to what he would have you to be. Let him demonstrate, through you, what he can do.

The next part of your moral inventory involves your sexual relationships. Our sexuality is God-given, and should therefore never by used lightly or selfishly, nor should it be despised or loathed, for it is good.

1. List the names of those with whom you've had a sexual relationship.

2. In each relationship, were you selfish or unselfish?

3. In each relationship, were you honest or dishonest?

4. In each relationship, were you considerate or inconsiderate?

5. In each relationship, did you hurt anyone (yourself, the person, others)?

6. In each relationship, did you justifiably arouse jealousy, suspicion, or bitterness?

7. Looking back at each relationship, was it, on the whole, a positive or a negative experience for you?

For the final part of our moral inventory, we will be looking at some personality defects—an imperfection or shortcoming of our character. Not everyone will have all these defects, or at least not to the same degree. But in all honesty, review your life, looking for examples of when you displayed each defect. Then write down examples of those that bother you the most.

1. Intolerance—"unwillingness or inability to accept others' opinions, beliefs, or behavior."

2. Minimizing—"making less of my behavior to make myself and others think I wasn't *that* bad."

3. Phoniness—"deceiving, insincere, sham, fake, not being genuine; it includes emotional phoniness."

4. Selfishness—"too concerned with my own welfare or interests, having little or no concern for others; what *I* want is the most important thing!"

5. Anger—"temper tantrums, rages, sulks, vindictiveness (getting even); all immature ways of responding to fear."

6. Covetousness—"having an unreasonable desire for things we should not or did not have."

7. Denial—"refusal to think about or hear about or admit things I did."

8. Pride—"a form of dishonesty, that is, acting, boasting, or pretending to myself and others that I was better than I was."

9. Alibis—"lies, reasons, excuses to justify my behavior."

10. Procrastination—"putting off to some future date something I should have done then."

11. Self-pity—"feeling sorry for myself, or continually grieving, which usually started with my blaming others for my troubles."

12. Impatience—"annoyance because of delay or opposition; 'I want what I want when I want it.'"

13. Shame—"feelings I had when I did not meet my own standards of behavior."

14. Guilt—"wrong doing; I did not meet others' standards of behavior."

STEP 5

Having completed your moral inventory, where are you now in terms of self-awareness and self-acceptance? What is your attitude toward change and growth? Are you committed to making some changes?

1. To help you get at these important questions, we encourage you to begin making your own plan for healthful living. As a suggestion, try listing *some* of your defects, those attitudes and behaviors that are causing you the most trouble. Then make some plans to deal with these specific defects. List some of your assets and incorporate them into your plan for personal growth. After you've made a plan, live it.

2. How do you feel about your new way of life? Do you show your gratitude to those who helped you build a new life? What are some ways you could express your gratitude right now? Can you see how feeling grateful can influence you in a positive way, and help you avoid the pitfalls of complacency, boredom, and depression?

3. Look back through your moral inventory, and begin a partial amends list—a list of people you have harmed. Later, when you are able, you can make amends to those people.

4. Being entirely ready means knowing specifically what we want God to remove and also what we want to replace our defect with. The following list of "little" virtues are building blocks:
   a. Courtesy
   b. Cheerfulness
   c. Order
   d. Loyalty
   e. Use of Time
   f. Punctuality
   g. Sincerity
   h. Caution in speech
   i. Kindness
   j. Patience
   k. Tolerance
   l. Integrity
   m. Balance
   n. Gratitude

5. Now list again all the defects that you've become "entirely ready" to have God remove. Opposite each one, write the virtue or building block that you want to replace it with.

STEP 6

Looking back at where we've been, and at where we still need to go, you may have already realized the next step. It is really impossible to ask God to remove our shortcomings unless we do so in all humility. Without some degree of humility, no addict can remain free of his or her addiction at all.

1. Look up the word "humility" in a dictionary, and write down its meaning. What does it mean to you?

2. List five specific ways you could exemplify or practice humility as a way of life.

3. Who is your Higher Power? Does he really have the power to heal you?

4. What stands between you and God that might keep him from removing all your shortcomings?

5. What do you expect will happen after you ask God to remove your shortcomings? Remember, some will be removed instantaneously, for others there may be a delay, some will be removed in a gradual process over much time, and some may not be removed at all.

6. Write a letter to God, and include the following:
   a. What you specifically ask him to remove.
   b. Why you need him to remove it.
   c. What you desire him to replace it with.
   d. Thank him for hearing your request and granting it.

   Scripture passages you may want to look up are 1 John 5:14-15; Philippians 4:6.

STEP 7

The final steps in our journey toward a healthful life cannot be written down. Rather, you need to act on what you have already written and discovered about yourself. You have already made a list of the people you have harmed; now, you need to make amends—except when to do so would injure them, yourself, or others.

God bless you with a successful recovery and a fruitful, healthy life.